LAST THINGS FIRST

(NEW WRITING SCOTLAND 13)

LAST THINGS FIRST

(NEW WRITING SCOTLAND 13)

Edited by

A.L. KENNEDY
and
JAMES McGONIGAL

with Meg Bateman (Gaelic Adviser)

Association for Scottish Literary Studies

Association for Scottish Literary Studies
c/o Department of English, University of Aberdeen
Aberdeen AB9 2UB

First published 1995

British Library Cataloguing in Publication Data

A CIP record for this book is available
from the British Library

ISBN 0–948877–27–8

Typeset by Roger Booth Associates, Hassocks, West Sussex

Printed by Cromwell Press, Melksham, Wiltshire

CONTENTS

INTRODUCTION

Hard on the heels of last year's sell-out edition comes *NWS 13*. Pervading themes of heat and sunlight have faded and now it seems that all the barometers from Bernera to Bearsden could be foiled by the storms sweeping in from Scotland's writers – their Atlantic highs and lows of the heart.

These characteristically Scottish shifts of atmosphere, at once extreme and subtle, make for modes of writing which are focused but never static. Riddling, wary, intense, oblique; the stories and poems of *NWS 13* ask large questions and put last things first.

By tradition the 'four last things' are death, judgement and heaven or hell. Why this year's writers are drawn to these extremes is anyone's guess. Perhaps their concerns are born out of a sharpening sense of political endings and beginnings, an increasing insecurity at local and international level, personal loss or gain.

Time and again water, the Celtic border marker between life and death, appeared in the four hundred or so submissions. Its imagery and symbolism flowed through diverse pieces: its influence both chaotic and life-giving. Naturally water marks our selection. A woman called Rapid exults in the fresh undercurrents of her tenement life; salt waves bring life and death to a fishing community. Freoch swims his legendary pool and a fish-eating car takes off from a sea cliff. The writing is filled with shock and delight.

Where is heaven in all of this? It seems to be all about us potentially. It is glimpsed in moments when we 'give back some brightness', or find life returned to us in love or unaccountable escape, or when the truthful witness of accurate writing redeems what was lost.

The last judgement fell to us and presented more difficulty than last year. Our problem was not so much one of who to let in as of who to leave out. Space and time are sadly not unlimited in *New Writing Scotland* and we had to assess new and established writers in differing languages with a range of issues and cultures to speak from. We were not exactly separating sheep from goats, more trying to keep a shared sense of identity amongst our whole flock. This all took time and we apologise for the perhaps purgatorial pains of waiting and even rejection. Next year in *NWS 14*? We hope so.

One piece in particular, which encompasses both first and last impressions, is worth noting. 'Prologue to the New Year' is the first publication of a section from an early journal by the esteemed prose writer Elspeth Davie who died not long ago. Her developing voice and eager mind recorded here will touch those who recall the insight and grace of her later work.

A.L. Kennedy
James McGonigal
August 1995

NEW WRITING SCOTLAND 14

Submissions are invited for the fourteenth annual volume of *New Writing Scotland*, to be published in 1996, from writers resident in Scotland or Scots by birth or upbringing. Poetry, drama, short fiction or other creative prose may be submitted but not full-length plays or novels, though self-contained extracts are acceptable. The work must be neither previously published nor accepted for publication and may be in any of the languages of Scotland.

Submissions should be typed on one side of the paper only and the sheets secured at the top-left corner. Each individual work should be clearly marked with the author's name and address.

Submissions should be accompanied by two stamped addressed envelopes (one for a receipt, the other for return of MSS) and sent by **31 January 1996 (not before November 1995)** to:

Catherine Mc Inerney
Managing Editor, NWS
ASLS
c/o Dept of English
Taylor Building
University of Aberdeen
Aberdeen AB9 2UB
Tel: 01224 272634

Donald Adamson

LAST THINGS

The milestones before a death
are the termini, the last times of things –
the final, datable instances
of routines, chores, small pleasures.

Like plainclothes policemen
they mingle with the crowd, so casual, disguised
in the jeans and jumpers
worn by a hundred previous occasions.

They hang no banners: *Congratulations,*
your last visit to Safeway, or
Happy never-to-be-repeated walk
along the shore road.

There are no dramas. The people, too,
the acquaintances bumped into
and said hello to and never seen again,
don't scream 'Make the most of me.'

Maybe the universe should end like that:
after the earth has written its Christmas cards,
or the galaxy come home
from a package holiday

or the cosmos gone for a stroll
and sniffed the perfume of birch leaves,
the first ones, that in the ordinariness
of spring's routines would always be there.

LUCID

Just as in a dream you dash frantically
laden with luggage down an impossible length
of street, Paris it might be, joining the queue
at the ticket office, the train about to leave,
the last carriage pulling away, you run for it –
a sprint, a leap ...

(But even as it begins, the waking mind
bawls *Achtung* and goose-steps you away,
leaving a sense of something that continues
elsewhere, for others, on a journey
to no dream-land, but to a reality,
a Midi beyond access or imagining.)

... so I wished for one senile and dying
such an awakening that she would leap
into unconsciousness and the lucidity
of inanimate stuff without hope or need, a spray
Creation shook from its own shaggy fur,
or that she'd see flash by the ruined arches
of ancient aqueducts, chalk escarpments
whiter than angels' robes, and poplar trees,
her sleep unbroken, no waking at all.

John Aberdein

ANDY TAWSE

Fine tae be thirlt tae historie even if the maist ye dae is grup till hir fleein cloaktails an cry mercy. Sae Peem thocht fan they tellt'm that Straloch College wis commandeerit bi Cumberland for Reidcoat quartirs eftir the '45. The Butcher o Culloden: aye there wis still butchers alive an weil an teachin at Straloch fan Peem went there.

Queer bugger o a place it wis, weil it hid tae be tae malform loons intae the petty rulers o Aiberdeen an twal mile roon. Vrocht iron gates it boastit, an a vrocht iron hairt, aa twistit wi curlicues an mottoes, *Ad Artem Omne Magister, Haud at them Dominie.* Plus a lang bonny drive aa til itsel, wi fine trig turf an greetin willaws, an at the end o't a blackent stane fortress, wi astricled windas, that made Stevenson's Hoose o Shaws seem like an E&M showroom. But Peem got on aaricht, like a skunk merkit wi the fite stripe o clivverness. Ony dunderheid got chowed up tho, the best ee culd dae jist sputten oot again like papir-mashy.

Like fan Mannie Green that taucht French got haud o a muckle leerup o a loon fae a Cooncil estate an gied him laldy. *Read the line, Duncan.* The laddie curlt ees left paa up tae ficher wi ees glesses. *Donny-moy... donny-moy...* We've had that bit. Wirds cam in a rummle *Donny-moy ... dyeuks gattox seal voo plate.*

Sleekit Greener upflappit ees elbucks aince, twice, hitchin comfy ees bleck goun aroon'm. *And again, Duncan, in French if you please?* A murmuration o loons tryan tae gie their Davie a haun *Moi, min... it's moi... moi.* *Donny-mwaa dyeuks gattox seal voo plate* it wis nane better. The upflap aince again, like a nesty shag perch-foo o fish at Girdleness. *French French I meant Duncan, not Mastrick French. Don't you realise the A class is supposed to contain the brains of the population, the future the world looks up to? And you come shambling in here* Duncan hid a curve in ees spine fae birth *and talk like a bus-conductor? Who is this Donny Mwaa, a sort of Chinese Highlander? And gattox – an early machine-gun maybe? – for the rest of us is gateaux. Don't you eat gateaux in Mastrick then?* Duncan's Da hid droont aff Murmansk. *Listen, boy: Donnez-moi deux gateaux, s'il vous plait. And stand up straight, you're like a human question mark.* An ee swung ees back on the sairmade loon an wis for seekin the tap o the cless, as tho tae say that bleckdookers wid raither ony day saumon nor shitey sadies fae Torry Docks.

Peem luikit doon in disgust, giean hauf a chance ee wid hiv vrappit ees leddir skweelbag roon Greener's smarmy phiss. Sae fan Mr Green spiert'm an easy-peasy ane, ee luikit clean throu the poppination an said *Don't know, sir* an *Don't know, sir* tae the next twa spierins an aa, sae that the mannie suld ken ee wis bein sent tae Cove till ee'd quelled ees spite. But ee wis stukken wi that name, Davie: they shoutit oot *Query Merk! Query Merk!* in the corridors tae mak'm turn roon.

Och, there wis the odd gweed teacher an aa, like Smiler Miles, the wee Latin mannie wi the reid matash, ee wid say *And can anyone tell me what Julius Caesar said when they stabbed him in turn till he fell on the Capital steps? No? ETCH! ye Brute!* Or *Let's conjugate amare, future tense. Amabo, I will love; amabis, you will love; amabit, she's keen!* Jist daft translations an transmogrifications, fine for a cackle, an aye wi Smiler ye got yir breath, specially an if ye'd jist hid Andy Tawse at the vera tap o the skweel.

Young Andy hid a room aneath the roof, wi a laich ceilin, aa covit, three dizzen o desks, a bleckboord an a scud. Fit mair culd ee wint? The mannie wis sae muckle in luve wi Maths, an himsel, that ee daunsit aboot the front o the class, fleerishin ees gounie ootower ees shouders like Dracula wi St Vitus, dashin aff a dizzen quadratics or fitivver on the boord, syne birlin an beamin at the blue-blazert battalion. *Follow, boys? Good. Top of 19 to the bottom of 21, at home for Thursday.*

But eftir the first term Tawser twiggit that mair nor hauf ees battalion were scrimshankers, they were only toyin wi their geometrie like kittlins teasin baas o oo in front the fire. Weil Pandy Andy wid nivver pit up wi that, a spankin-new dominie wintin tae mak ees mark an mebbe get a bigger placie doon bi the staffroom. Sae next Tuesday ee dustit the fite chack fae ees paums, an cam oot wi fresh orders. *Books away. Jotters open. A clean page. Write out the definition:* – ee gave each row its luik – *parallel straight lines.*

Peem vrote wi ees rare gowd Parker, that wis afore ee chored qweeksiller in the tap o'r an meltit the nib *Parallel straight lines are straight lines such that, no matter how far they are produced in either direction, will never meet.*

An fine young Mr Tawse, wi ees locks slickt back, strode throu the banks o desks like a heron eftir troot cryan *OUT!... OUT!... Yes... Yes... OUT!...* Fae bank tae bank. *Yes* tae Peemie *OUT!* tae The Human Question Mark. *OUTDuncanyesyou! YES, parallel has 3 l's but NOT where you've put them!*

An the line o defaulters wid sune wynd back fae the dominie's desk, alang the front o the cless an up the side, aince richt back tae the prison-winda wi aa the wee squarrs like Craiginches. An fan ee'd inspectit ivvery jotter tae see fit loons culdna parrot oot their Euclid tae the last dot an letter, weil sicna lads hid tae be shown better weys. An ee kept ees scud, it wis braid an thin, like a coo's tail that hid been flattent bi a steamroller, rollit ower ees shouder aneath ees gounie, like the Marshall o Dodge City hidin ees gun. Weil there wis nae dodgin fit cam next, fower thwacks apiece an back tae yir seat, Andy Tawse breezin on like a millie that wid have connacht ten Quixotes.

Syne on tae the next inquisition, aboot points, perpendiculars, or foo did ye preeve twa triangles congruent, supposin ye were in a hurry for that ivver? The lines o loons nivver gettin ony shorter, an neither belt nor mannie seemin tae wear oot, it cast a fair gloom on the wiks, ivvery Tuesday an Thursday.

Peem wid wauk at a five in the mornin, an sheen the rubber leerie aneath the bedclaes, connin ees theorems til they were near aa prentit roon the inside o ees scherp neep. Forbye, Tawser didna hae een in the back o ees heid an ye culd aye gie antrin keeks inside yir desk. But Humphy Davie wis ployless, ee jist got warse an warse, the sairer ees paum, the bigger sotter ees Pythagoras, til ee stertit tae stutter an culdna say ees name. *D... D... David D... Duncansir,* the loon wis a bigger wreck nor the traaler oot at Black Dog. An of coorse the twa McVies

were as bad, the gadgie wi the gless ee, an the ane wi the cock
they caad Tosser. Ae double period it seemed they were vyin
each wi ither fa culd score the maist pandies wi Tawser's tawse,
an it wis a draa, they culd hardly get past twenty apiece bi the
sacont bell. Weil they hid sweemin in the wee pool richt eftir, in
they dove, baith Glesser an Tosser, an fan their hauns hut the
wattir, up cam fower cloods o steam, ye suld have seen it.

Eftir a month an a hauf there wir only three o the lads
hidna felt the wecht o Tawser's belt. An Peem's faither heard o
the thing, an bein that ees ain loon hidna been scuddit, ee felt
it stude far better for him tae ging breengin up on appointment wi the Heidie, an tell auld Ebeneezer it jist wisna on, this
malagarousin o First Year laddies as tho they were inower a
barbt-wire camp. Ees Da nivver lat on muckle, nivver a billy
tae boast, but a wik or twa eftirwards, for decency's sake, the
tawse wis pittan ta-ta til its bed an the terror wis bye wi.

Tho nae afore Andy tuik tae haltin the period wi time an
tae spare, pittan ees smowkin scud back in its howster, an
comin tae sit aa nicie-nicie on ane o the front loons' desks. An
fit Bonny Brylcreem wintit tae news aboot wis Easter, nae the
Crucifixion for a wonder, but the skweel's skiin trippie tae
Switzerlaun, open tae First Year an aabuddy, only thirty-five
pun a heid, promist tae be a hale dose better this year than
last, an wi Yourstruly Candybully helpin aabuddy tae hae fun.
Loons that widna have kent a ski fae a palin post nor an
avalanche fae a burst bolster ran trippin ower their bags tae
pit their names doon, saft eneuch tae think their subscrievin
tae Tawser's free Easter wid win pardon next time they were a
bit harum-scarum on the auld theorems. Peem didna. Ee kent
it wis a swick. Ee kent there wisna thirty-five pun lying aboot
the sideboord at hame an nivver wid be, the only thing Swiss
in the hoose wis Ma's Swiss Mulk Toffee made wi fit they likit
tae ca Condemned Mulk. Foo Humphy Davie Duncan got tae
ging ee nivver did ken, ees Ma that went aa winter trauchlin
fae the Broo tae the Auld Breider wi barely a scarf tae hir heid.

An that wid have been aa aboot it, ninety-nine per cent o
the inmates gaain tae Zermatt aa o a suddent, the beltin stop-
pin like a schouer o hail scuddin bye, an aabuddy as gweed at
Maths as a tribe o Greeks.

Then aboot the stert o April Peem wis postin ees papirs
throu the Urquhart doors fan ee saa in the *Evening Express* a

gey sair bittie: *City Boy in Holiday Horror*, there wis aye somethin. Fisslan back throu the Alps on the chookchook, ane o the Straloch pairty hid mebbe gogglit at the sign *Ne pas se pencher par la fenetre* but sure as fate that's fit ee'd deen, yarkit the sash an stukken ees heid oot the winda. Haein a fine time ee wis, skiffan parallel tae the cliff an guffan the weet rock, fan it suddantlie nerrat, there wis a maist affa thump, an the derk gaed adirlin like the Divvil's dock. Hid tae be the Human Question Mark of coorse, hid tae be Davie.

They tellt Peem eftir that fit wis left o the lump fell back an hut Tawser. But nae till they were oot the tunnel did the young shavers lat skirl: they must've thocht aa the King's Horse hid flasht past wi sabres birlin. *Puir Tawser* they said *ees phiss gaed pure fite... fite as dooshit... fite as a doo's breist!*

An Daft Duncan's mither made a sicht o hirsel for months aboot the toon, scoofin vodka in Ma's an The Silver Slipper, aye traipsin up an doon Schoolhill, till she tuik the scarfsquarr fae hir heid, the cotton belt fae hir coat, an hung hirsel on the auld vrocht iron gates.

Pamela Beasant

TEN LINES OF GREETING AND GOODBYE

Blood drains from your forming shape;
dying, you bob in the one soft place
you want to occupy in the world.
No harsh light, hard surfaces for you,
banging out your heart and soul
against life's drums and bricks.
Slowly you let your hold slip,
slide out dead through the birthing place,
over the brink of your long, black space;
weaned, before your captive mouth can suck.

Annette Berman

FROECH IN THE DARK POOL
From an 8th century Irish legend

She said to Froech, 'Do not come out
till you bring me a bunch of rowan;
so lovely are the berries.'
He turned to break a spray
and carried it swimming on his back.

No sight was again more beautiful
than his pale skin in that dark pool;
his black hair, blue eyes
and the branch with scarlet berries
that flamed on his throat and white face ...

Niall Brownlie

CAITRIONA

Sgeulachd mun ghort anns An Aetiòp

Agus cluinnidh sibh cogaidhean, agus tuairisgeul chogaidh-
ean: thugaibh an aire nach bi sibh fo amhluadh: oir is èiginn
do na nithean sin uile teachd gu crìch, ach chan eil a' chrìoch
ann fhathast.

Oir èiridh cinneach an aghaidh cinnich, agus rìoghachd an
aghaidh rìoghachd: agus bidh gortan, agus plàighean, agus
crithean-talmhainn ann am mòran àitean. Agus chan eil annta
seo uile ach toiseach thruaighean.

An sin bheir iad thairis sibh chum amhghair agus marbh-
aidh iad sibh, agus bidh fuath aig gach uile chinneach dhuibh
air sgàth m' ainme-sa.

Mata 24. 6 gu 9.

On chiad là san deachaidh Caitrìona don àrd sgoil, b' i a
glòir-mhiann a bhith na lighiche mar a h-athair roimhpe. Ach
mo chreach, chaidh esan a mharbhadh an tubaist càir nuair a
bha i na caileig bhig.

Bha i gleusda am fòghlam, is an uair a bha i rèidh san àrd
sgoil chaidh i do dh' oilthigh Dhùn-Eideann, rud nach robh
soirbh is gun na màthair ach banntrach. Ged a bha an cùrsa
cruaidh, chaidh i ris an fhòghlam gu dealasach is rè ùine
dh'fhàg i Dùn Eideann le sreath litrichean ri h-ainm.

Nuair a bha i rèidh dhan oilthigh chaidh i don Taigh-
eiridinn Roghail an Glaschu far an do chuir i seachad dà
bhliadhna na lighiche-taighe agus tri bliadhna na làimh-lèigh.
Ach cha robh i sona is thug i Muile oirre far an d' fhuair i co-
roinn an raon-dèiligidh. Ged a bha tlachd mhòr aice sna daoine
is anns an eilean cha do ghabh a h-inntinn gu clos is bha i a'
sìor-iarraidh an nì sin nach robh ri fhaotainn – sàsachadh na
dreuchd. Dè bha i a' sireadh, cha robh fios aice, ach bha i
dearbhte nach robh e seunte fo choilltean is àrd-bheanntan
Mhuile.

Nuair a bheireadh i sgrìob dhachaigh is a thogadh i a'
cheist ri màthair, theireadh ise, "Chan eil ann, eudail, ach
smuain – sgàil fhaoin a thèid seachad ri tìm."

"Dhùraiginn gum b' i sin an fhìrinn, a mhàthair," theireadh
i gu dubhach.

Ach mar a tha an sean-fhacal ag ràdh, 'A' chlach tha air
thurraman tuitidh i uaireigin' is fhuair i fuasgladh bhon staing
san robh i air feasgar àraidh 's i a' coimhead air prògram mun
ghoirt san Aetiòp. Dhrùidh na deilbh de phàisdean – am
brùthan air at leis a' chaoile is neul an acrais air an gruaidhean
– gu mòr oirre.

"Seo far a bheil m' fhàgail-sa is chan ann am Muile agus
seo far am bi mi a dh' aithghearr," thubbairt i na h-inntinn.
Thug i cuairt dhachaigh a dh'innseadh da màthair na bha na
rùn. Ged a bha ise glè dhiombach dhith, an nì a bha na ceann,
bha e na casan is cha tug i cluas dhi. Thill i do Mhuile is leig i
dhith a dreuchd.

Thug i oirre gu Lunnainn far an d' rinn i ullachadh airson
a dhol a dh'Afraca. A' tadhal air a' Chrois Dheirg, fhuair i
cungaidhean-leighis is nithean eile a bhitheadh feumail san
obair a bha roimhpe is a' chuid nach d' fhuair i an sin, fhuair i
aig Oxfam. Ged a bha i dearbhte gun robh iomadh cruadal is
bristeadh-dùil an lùib an t-siubhail, b' e seo a rùn is bha e an
urra rithe fhèin a roghainn a dhèanamh dheth. Mun do shearg
a' ghealach bha i anns An Aetiòp.

B' ann aig a' port-adhair a fhuair i a' chiad bhristeadh-dùil.
A rèir coltais bha seachad air tri cheud mìle eadar i is a ceann-
uidhe. Is bha fathann a' dol gun robh an rathad mòr fo
smachd reubalach, gun inneal-giùlain san àite a bha deònach a
shiubhal. Cha robh ach aon slighe eile fosgailte agus b' e sin
thar frith-rathaidean is gharbhlach. Tri ceud mìle a dh'astar,
gun modh siubhail ri fhaighinn. Thàinig i gu 'n cho-dhùnadh
nach robh nì foipe ach tilleadh dhachaigh is, a' sileadh nan
deur, chuir i a h-aghaidh air an taigh-òsda far an robh cuid na
h-oidhche a' feitheamh oirre.

Air dhi a dhol a-steach don t-seòmar-shearraidh laigh a sùil
air gille òg gasda an èideadh màidseir na shuidhe na aonar aig
bòrd. Nuair a chunnaic e na deòir, dh'èirich e na còmhdhail,
ag ràdh, "Dè tha cur ort? Tha thu air dhroch chàradh a rèir
coltais."

"Agus cò thusa?" dh' fharraid i dheth gu farranach.

"O, gabh mo leisgeul. Is mise Calum MacSuain à Beinn na
Faoghla."

"Is dè a thug an taobh seo thu? Bheil thu san t-Seirbhis
Sheòltach?"

"Chan eil. Is e tha annam ach saighdear-tuarasdail. Obair chruaidh gun teagamh, ach chan eil an t-saothair gun duais aig uairibh."

"Airgead fola! Is e cùis-dèisinn a tha annad," thubhairt i, a' cur bus mòr oirre.

"Tog ort! Nach tu a tha frithearra?" thubhairt e, a' dèanamh snodha gàire. "Thig is gabh cofaidh còmhla rium nuair a bhios tu rèidh. Ma dh'fhaoite gun cuir e fonn nas fheàrr ort. Tha thu an cruaidh fheum air cuideachd mur eil mi air mo mhealladh."

"Tapadh leat." Is fheàrr cuireadh pìobaire na bhith gun chuireadh idir.

"Is e do bheatha e," thubhairt e, a' leigeil seachad a cabaireachd.

"Bidh mi rèidh an leth-uair. Ged nach tu mo rogha cuideachd, chan eil taghadh aig tè-na-faoighe." Is a' tionndadh air a sàil thug i an seòmar-ionnlaid oirre. Bha i air a h-ais an leth-uair mar a gheall i is rinn iad le chèile air a' bhàr-chofaidh.

"Rudeigin nas làidire na cofaidh an toiseach?" thubhairt Calum gu coibhneil.

"Thigeadh glainne branndaidh rium, mas e do thoil e."

Bha e air ais an tiota, dà ghlainne branndaidh aige is air dhaibh suidhe thubhairt e, "innis dhomh cò thu is dè a thug thu air astar cian mar seo?"

"Is mise an Dotair Caitrìona NicAoidh à Eisdeal is thàinig mi don Aetiòp a dhèanamh foire air na truaghain a tha acrach, easlan is ris a' bhàs.

"Misean ionmholta gun teagamh is tha thu rid mholadh. Ach tha campa nam fogarrach seachad air trì cheud mìle air falbh."

"Sin a chuala mi aig a' phort-adhair. Is on nach eil seòl agam air an turas a ghabhail is mòr m' eagal gun èigin dhomh tilleadh an taobh an tàinig mi. "Chan eil mi, a rèir coltais, ach a' ruagadh nan caorach don dris."

"Tha Range Rover agamsa," thubhairt e, nach dh' fheumadh tu tuilleadh mòr is sin a dhol air turas mar seo. Tha an t-slighe làn gàbhaidh is cha ann bhon fhàsach no bho bheathaichean allta na machrach a-mhàin. Bheil sgil agad air airm-theine?"

"Chan eil." "Is ann a leigheas is chan ann a chiùrradh no a mharbhadh a thàinig mi an seo."

"Is mòr m' eagal gu bheil beatha is bàs a' siubhal an cois a

chèile san tìr seo. Mas e a tha nad mhiann sealladh fhaighinn
air Cheithir Marcaichean an Taisbeanaidh, seo an t-àite. Bheil
airgead agad?"
  "Tha cuimse. Tha thu a' cur sgreamh orm. Chan eil mi
gad iarraidh fhèin no an Range Rover an asgaidh."
  "Sin ort fhèin, a laochag! Is fìor thoigh leam nighean òg,
mheanmnach. Is duilich leam ach cha bhi an Rover deiseil gu
ceann cola-deug. Ach on a tha fios agam a-nis air ceann do
sheud 's do shiubhail, caithidh sinn an t-sìde gad fhòghlam an
cluich arm-theine. Bheir sin dhuit an cothrom air thu fhèin a
thoirt às san fhàsach gharbh seo. Cofaidh?"
  "Chòrdadh sin air leth math rium."
  Feadh 's a bha iad a' gabhail na cofaidh, rèitich iad ceann-
latha gu dol an ceann leasan an cluich arm-theine. Gun robh i
aineolach sa chleas, bha sin follaiseach, ach bha i dealasach, is
aig ceann a' chola-deug rachadh aice air neach a sgathadh sìos
gu clis. Is bha Calum dearbhte gun dèanadh i sin gun ath-
smuain is gun iochd nan tigeadh cùisean gu h-aon 's gu dhà.
  Mar a bu mhotha a bha e na cuideachd, b' ann a bu
mhotha a bha a spèis dhi a' fàs. Ach chum e a smuain aige
fhèin. Ged a bha i càirdeil gu leòr bha i an seagh eile fuar, fada
às is cha do nochd i riamh dha an taobh eile de a nàdar. A
dh'aindeoin sin bha e cinnteach gun robh leanmhainn a
thaobh-eigin a' fàs eatorra.
  Nuair a bha gach càil gu am miann thog iad orra chun na
garbhlaich, Caitrìona le ùrnaigh air a bilean. Nuair a fhuair
iad air farsaingeachd an fhàsaich, dh'fharraid i dheth dè cho
fada 's a bheireadh an turas.
  "Tri làithean air a' chuid as lugha. Tha a t-slighe cus is cò
aige tha fios dè na gàbhaidhean a tha romhainn," fhreagair e.
  "Tha an dealbh-thìr seo mar aghaidh na gealaich," thubhairt i. "Ma tha Muile nan Craobh gorm, fàsail, tha an t-àite
seo dustach, lom – dìthreabh fhalamh gun Dia, gun ainmhidh,
gun daoine."
  Na toir fìdeadh gu bheil i lom, fàs, gun daoine, eudail."
  "Na bi tarraing asam," thubhairt i gu biorach. "Cha
tigeadh an luch beò an seo, gun tighinn air duine."
  "Feuch ort, a bhrònag," thubhairt e gu cas. "Tha ceannaircich ghuineach air fàrsan an fhàsaich seo a thruailleadh thu is,
an uair a dh' fhàsadh iad searbh dhiot, a ghearradh do sgòrnan
bho chluais gu cluais. Is mur eil mi air mo mhealladh, tha iad ri
faireadh oirnn air a' cheart mhionaid."

B' ann air madainn an ath là a fhuair iad a' chiad aiteal de
na marcaichean. "Cò mheud a tha ann?" dh'fharraid e.
"Suas air fichead mur eil mi air mo mhealladh."
"Cum san amharc iad mas urrainn dhuit. Ach na biodh
iomagain ort. Cumaidh iad san dubhar is cha bhuail iad oirnn
gu tig fionnarachd an fheasgair. Tha a' ghrian a' dìreadh agus
is fheàrr dhuinn àite teàrainte is seasgar a lorg ro àine an là."
Goirid an dèidh, thug e gearradh tarsaing an fhàsaich gu
bun nam beann far an do lorg e còs cumhaing ri cùl grèine is ri
aghaidh gaoithe, còs air a dhìon le cas-chreagan thar nach
streapadh muncaidh gun tighinn air duine. An dèidh an Range
Rover a chur às an rathad, ghabh iad biadh, is an sin chaidh
iad air faire fo dhubhar nan creag. "Ma dh'fhaoite gun do
chaill iad lorg oirnn?" thubhairt i gu dòchasach nuair a chuir i
grèim fon aisinn.
"Gum bitheadh tu cho gòrach, mo laogh geal. Is math sin a
tha fios aca far a bheil sinn." fhreagair Calum. "'S e tha againn
an seo ach falach fead, a ghràidh. Mar a thubhairt mi, cha toir
iad ionnsaigh oirnn gu fionnarachd an fheasgair. Is an uair a
bhuaileas iad thig iad, a' marcachd air mire-chuthaich. Is fhada
on là sin anns am b' eòl dhòmhsa an cuid thratan. Tha iad cho
carach ris an t-sionnach. Bi air d' earalas ach na leig urchair
gus am bi iad an raon-bualaidh."
Sin mar a chaith iad an là, a' feitheamh is a' faire. Agus
mar a thubhairt Calum b' fhìor. B' ann air an fheasgar a
bhuail iad – ladhran nan each aca a' cur duslach an fhàsaich
na smùid don iarmailt. Nuair bha iad am beul urchair air
falbh, dhòirt teine guineach a' bhàis à cùl nan creagan –a'
sgathadh each is mharcaichean gu talamh gus an robh seachad
air deichnear nan laighe gun phlosg air a' ghainneimh.
Nuair a chunnaic càch an companaich am fuar ghlac a'
bhàis, thàir iad às ach aon a-mhàin. Chum esan air, a' dèanamh
calg-dhìreach air Caitrìona, daga gleuste na làimh. A rèir
coltais, cha robh dol às aice air. Ach a' leughadh a' chunnairt,
chaidh Calum san eadraigean – a' sgathadh sìos a' cheannairc-
ich ged a bhuail peilear sa ghualainn e.
Nuair a thàinig Caitrìona thuice fhèin 's a chunnaic i an
fhuil air lèine a companaich, thug i leum aisde ga ionnsaigh, a'
sracadh na lèine a leigeil ris an lot. Ach an dèidh sùil a thoirt
air, chunnaic i nach b' e droch lot a bha ann, oir chaidh am
peilear glan tron ghualainn gun chnàmh a mhilleadh. A' dol
chun a' Range Rover, fhuair i ìoc-chòmdaich, pilleachan

moirfin is ola-ungaidh. Ghoil i an sin uisge is air dhi an lot fhailceadh, ghabh i aige is thug i dha ann-stealladh de phenisiolin agus pile moirfin.

"Tapaidh leat airson gabhail aig mo ghualainn," thubhairt e an dèidh dhi a ghàirdean a chur an stail.

"'Se do bheatha e. Ach is tu fhèin a tha airidh air cliù is air taing. Mura b' e do ghiùlan gaisgeil fhèin, dh'fhoghain am fear ud dhomh." Is ag èirigh air a corra-biod thug i pòg dha. Ged a bha buille throm aig a chridhe, chaidh aige air e fhèin a cheannsachadh.

"Saoil thusa, tha i daonna an dèidh sin 's na dhèidh." thubhairt e fo anail nuair a chaidh i gu cùl an Rover. "Dè nis?" dh'fharraid e nuair a thill i. "Chan urrainn dhòmhsa an carbad a' stiùireadh air leth-làimh.

"Na biodh iomagain sam bith ort, a bhalaich. Gabhaidh mise às laimh an dràibheadh gus an ruig sinn ar ceann-uidhe. Is iomadh là sin a shiubhail mi rathaidean cam, cumhaing Mhuile le Land Rover."

"Nach ann dhomh a rug an cat an cuilean nuair a thog thu ceann?" thubhairt e, a' fanaid oirre.

"Nach buidhe dhuit an teanga sgaiteach a tha agad?" fhreagair i, ag amharc air gu nimheil. Is a' leum gu cùl na cuibhle, dh'èigh i: "Greas ort, a shlaoid. Chan e seo Beinn na Faoghla. Tha e uainn a bhith air falbh mun till na samhanaich a theich le feachd eile air an cùl. Ciamar a tha do ghualann?"

"Cràiteach, ach cha dèan sin dragh sam bith dhuitsa. Tha thu cruaidh-chridheach is gun iochd," thubhairt e, a' suidhe ri taobh, drèin na mallachd air.

"Feuch thusa!" thubhairt i, a' bearradaireachd. "Am Màidsear MacSuain duilich air a shon fhèin, ach na bitheadh cùram ort, thig thu uaith'. Is i a' chungaidh leighis as goirte as mò tha dèanamh feuma."

Ged a bha a seanachas mar rinn snathaid na fheòil, bha a làthaireachd ri thaobh a' fadadh sradag a' ghaoil na bhroilleach is bha a chridhe a' cagar ris, "Paisg nad bhroilleach i." Ach bha a chogais ag ràdh: "Amadain ghòraich! Nach tu tha mìr às do chiall is fios is cinnt agad nach motha leatha thu seach am fear a rinn a' phrais-bheag."

Cha deachaidh iad fada air an t-slighe nuair a theann an t-uisge san einnsean air goil is b' fheudar dhaibh stad. Air do Chalum a' bhonaid a thogail chunnaic e air ball gun robh crios a' ghaotharain briste. "Dè nis? dh'fharraid e, a chridhe na shlugan. Chan eil crios eile againn, is ged a bhitheadh chan eil mi comasach air a chur an grèim."

"Fuirich ort, a bhalaich," thubhairt i, a' deanamh gu cùl a' charbaid.

"Càite bheil thu a' dol no dè a tha nad cheann?" ghairm e às a dèidh.

"Cha bhi sin 's do shuipear agad," thàinig am freagairt. An ùine ghoirid thill i, stocainn nàidhlein na làimh.

"Necessitas est mater inventionis," thubhairt i gu bradalach.

"A ghloic gun chèill, dè a' bhruidhinn gun tùr a tha sin agad," thubhairt e gu feargach. "Cha robh mi dèidheil riamh air bradag àrdanach air bheagan cèille. Agus rud eile dheth, chan fhada a mhaireas an stocainn mar chrios."

"'S i a bhò as miosa sa bhuaile is cruaidhe geum. Tha facal mòr agad ach tha cainnt saor. 'S e dearbhadh a' ghnothaich a bhuil. An i an teas is adhbhar dod sheanachas gun bhrìgh. Bheirinn comhairle ort leigeil dha air a' mhionaid. Tha do ghàbhaidheachd gam chur thuige." Agus gun fhacal eile chrom i fon bhonoid is chaidh i an sàs san obair a bha roimhpe. Mun do ruith ach cairteal na h-uarach, bha iad deas glan gu siubhal. Rè na h-ùine bha Calum na shuidhe sa cheabain – fìor dhroch sheòl air a bhrìgh gun d' fhuair i smachd air.

B' ann an uair a fhuair i air ceann an rathaid a mhothaich i don stùic a bha air. "Ciamar a tha a' ghualann a-nis?" dh'fharraid i dheth.

"Chan eil adhbhar gearain," fhreagair e am fìor dhroch shunnd.

"Is dè fon ghrèin a tha cur ort ma ta?"

"Chan eil ach cho…"

"Cum ort! na bi cho diùid, is dona a tha e tighinn dhuit."

"Is e a bha mi dol a ràdh nuair a chuir thu stad orm cho gleusda 's a tha thu fhèin 's gun annad ach am boireannach."

"Male chauvinist pig!" fhreagair i a' dèanamh clap gàire.

Tràth san oidhche air a' cheathramh là thug iad a-mach an ceann-uidhe, campa aig bun nam beann. On a bha iad cho sgìth ris na coin, thog iad na teantaichean is an dèidh dhi gabhail aig a ghualainn le bann ghlan, ghabh iad grèim bìdh. Thug aid an sin na pocannan cadail orra, toilichte gun robh an turas seachad.

Air an làrna-mhàireach, bha Caitrìona air a buinn gu brisg mun robh an là ach a' glasadh. An dèidh cofaidh maidne chuir i cuairt air a' champa, far an robh na seallaidhean a bha fa comhair a' cur gris tro a feòil. Anns gach cùil is fròig bha daoine nan sìneadh a' dol a dhìth leis a' chaoile.

Nan taic, bha pàisdean, ri uchd a' bhàis, a' deoghal air cìochan seasg is an fheadhainn a bu shine a' seargadh às le sgàird, a' chaitheamh, fiabhras is gach eucail eile a tha air gach àm a' siubhal cruaidh an lùib na gorta. Bha e follaiseach gun robh a' mhor-chuid de phlàighean na cruinne an seo fiù 's gu na cuileagan is na radain. Ged nach b' i boireannach cràbhach a bha innte, ar leatha gun robh guth na cluais ag ràdh: 'Eloi, Eloi, lama, sabachtani?' Lùb i sìos air a glùinean is dh'èigh i na càs: "Iosa! Thusa don lèir am fulangas, dèan eadar-ghuidhe air an son."

Thill i chun an teanta is, an dèidh grèim bracaist, chruinnich i leatha cungaidhean leighis is thill i a dhèanamh cobhair air na truaghain bhochd, bhreòite a bha nan laighe teann oirre. Ged a rinn i a dicheall, cha robh ann dhi an seagh ach saothair gun duais.

Am beul an fheasgair, thill i sgìth, airsneulach chun an teanta. Air dhi a dhol a-steach chunnaic i na laighe air an làr pàisde caileig don tug i antibiotaic na bu tràithe a latha. Na laighe na cois, bha a màthair an spàirn a' bhàis. Os an cionn, bha duine caol, neònach a' labhairt oibe. Faisg air bha poit shalach, dhubh às an robh boladh gràineil ag èirigh.

"Dè tha thu a' dèanamh, a dhaoir thrusdair!," dh' èigh i, fearg a' chuthaich oirre. "Thoir am blàr a-muigh ort air a' mhionaid!" Is a' toirt breaba san tòin dha, chuir i an ruaig air – a' phoit 's na bha innte teann air a shàil. Nuair a chuala Calum an ùbraid, thàinig e na chabhaig a choimhead air dè bha cur oirre.

"An aithne dhuit am fear-fuadain ud?" dh'fharraid i dheth gu feargach.

"Chunna mi e uair na dhà nas tràithe a latha. Is e a tha agad an siud ach Mahmoud, am feall-lighiche. 'S e a ghluais thu an seo ach cumhachdan an dorchadais. Bi air d' earail roimhe. Seall romhad air neo bidh do bhàs aige. Mhaslaich thu e am fianais na trèibh is chan fhaod e sin a' leigeil seachad. Seo agad daga is cum air do ghiùlan e gach uair."

Chaith i tri làithean eile a' freasdal air an luchd tinneis, a' dèanamh a dichill air faochadh a thoirt dhaibh. Ach cha robh i ach ag iarraidh maoraich ri muir-làn, oir bha iad a dol a dhìth nam ficheadan ge b' oil leatha.

Bha i fhèin a-nis an impis toirt thairis is air dhi dol dhachaigh anmoch air an fheasgar, thug i am poca cadail oirre. Ach eadar cadal is dùsgadh chual' i faram sracaidh is air dhi sùil a thoirt mun cuairt, chunnaic i san leus Mahmoud a' bualadh thuice, sgian na làimh.

Gun ath-smuain, tharraing i an daga is chuir i peilear an clàr-aodainn a leag fuar às a sheasamh e. Leum i an sin air a casan, is thug i ràn aisde. Bha Calum san teanta a' leughadh, ach nuair a chual' e an urchair is an ràn, thàinig e na chabhaig da h-ionsaigh. Nuair a nochd e, thug i dud leum aisde, a' tilgeil a dà làimh mu amhaich.

"Leig dhiot puinneag bheag ded bhoile eudail," thubhairt e gu socrach. "Cha robh dà rian agad air ach cur às dha. Tha mi mòr asad. Ach chan fhaod sinn an corp fhàgail an seo. Feumaidh sin bothan a chur air mun tig an trèibh mu mhullach ar cinn. Ma gheibh iad sinn an seo, bidh sinn an geall nach fhiach sinn."

Mu thruaighe! gum b' fheudar dhomh cur às dha." thubhairt i gu tùrsach.

"Cha leighis duilchinn an gnìomh, nì mò an nì aithreachas mall bonn feuma," thubhairt e gu frionasach.

An dèidh an corp a chur le stalla a bha faisg air a' champa, thug iad gu làr na teantaichean is sgioblaich iad leo gach goireas don Rover. "Bheil diseal gu leòr againn?" dh'fharraid i.

"Gu leòr is barrachd," fhreagair e gu mi-fhoighidneach.

"Is dè mun stocainn air a' ghaotharan?"

"Lorg mi crios eile an cùl an Rover an-dè is chuir mi an grèim e," fhreagair e. "Gabh gu cùl na cuibhle is gabh a-mach às seo aig peilear do bheatha.

"Mar as àill leat, a chaomhain," thubhairt i, a' cur a' charbaid fo uidheam.

Air an dara là ràinig iad bealach cumhaing far an robh còmhlan reubalach a' feitheamh am fàth, is cha b' ann a' marcachd a bha iad. Is e a bha aca an seo ach milisi gu gunnach, dagach le carbadan armachd. "Chan eil seòl againn air dol às orra," thubhairt Calum. "Feumaidh sinn gèilleachdainn dhaibh."

An ùine gheàrr bha iad fhèin 's an Rover an campa uaigneach eadar dà bheinn. An dèidh do na ceannaircich an slaodadh a-mach às a' charbad, chuir iad ceangal a' chaoil orra is thilg iad do theanta iad le freiceadan gam faire. Ach aig beul na h-oidhche, chaidh aig Caitrìona air Calum fhuasgladh.

"Thoir ràn asad," thubhairt e rithe, a' dol air falach aig fosgladh an teanta. Nuair a chual' am freiceadan an sgreuch, thug e roid a-steach ach le buille de chùl a bhoise rinn Calum coileach dubh dheth. An sin cheangail e e cho cruinn ri molt is leig e ma rèir Caitrìona. "Dèan air an Rover an deanna-nambonn. Bidh mise air m' ais cho luath 's a ghabhas dèanamh." Is a' glacadh a' ghunna a bha aig an fhreiceadan, rinn e a-mach às an teanta. "Càit' a bheil thu a' dol?" dh'èigh i às a dhèidh.

"Coma leatsa sin," fhreagair e, a' toirt a chinn fodha don duibhre. Rinn Caitrìona mar a dh'iarradh oirre ach bha i fo chùram mòr a thaobh a companaich. Ach an ceann tacain thill e le ceannard a' mhilisi na phrìosanach aige – daga cruaidh ri cùl a chinn.

"Gheibh an siad seo sinn sàbhailte às an staing sa bheil sinn," thubhairt e, ga sparradh an ceabain an Rover. Shìn e an sin an daga do Chaitrìona, ag ràdh, "Na toir do shùil dheth gus am faigh mi air a chùlaibh. Chan eil ann ach grèim air earball easgainne."

Nuair a fhuair e àite socrach air cùlaibh an reubalaich is an daga ri cùl a chinn, ghluais Caitrìona air falbh gu fàilidh. Nuair a thug iad a-mach a' chachaileith aig bun a' ghlinne, bha dithis fhreiceadan air faire. "Air do bheatha na leig ort gu bheil càil ceàrr," thubhairt Calum ris a' cheannard. "Abair riu gu bheil thu a' toirt leat Caitrìona gu campa eile."

Le eagal dearg a bheatha air, rinn an ceannairceach mar a dh'iarradh air. Is air do na freiceadain an geata fhosgladh dhaibh, fhuair Caitrìona farsaingeachd an fhàsaich fo a sròin is cha robh pilleadh oirre. An dèidh dhaibh mu astar deich mìle a chur eadar iad fhèin 's an campa, dh' iarr Calum oirre stad. "Gheibh sinn cuidhteas 's an saobhaire seo mun tèid sinn nas fhaide.

"Chan eil thu a' dol a chur às dha?" dh'fharraid i dheth fo iomagain.

"Cha robh sin nam bheachd idir. Ach cha dèan cuairt dan dìthribh beud air. Thig a chàirdean air a thòir nuair a thig ionndrain air." An dèidh sin chum iad orra, a' siubhal gu dian gus an d' ràinig iad an taigh-òsda a dh'fhàg iad o chionn còrr air cola-deug air ais.

"Tha mi mòr asad," arsa Calum rithe nuair a fhuair iad suidheachain san t-seòmar-shearraidh. Tha thu cruaidh, sgàirteil gun teagamh."

"Nach tu tha leam leat agus beulach?" fhreagair i. "Ach is minic a thàinig fealla-dhà gu fealla-trì."

Leig Calum seachad na thubhairt i is, an dèidh drama is cofaidh, chuir iad an cinn fopa, oir bha iad sgith, claoidhte.

Sa mhadainn a-màireach – an dèidh na bracaist – chaidh iad a-mach air sràid. "Càit' a-nis, a Chaluim?" dh'fharraid i. "Dhachaigh, càit' eile!" fhreagair e. "Is e sin a bha air m' aire nuair a thachair sinn."

"Is an ainn an Aigh, dè a bhuair thu gu falbh còmhla riumsa air a leithid de thuras."

"Gòraiche a' ghaoil, a luaidh. Dè eile?"

Sheas i aige, gun fhios aice dè a theireadh i no cò an taobh a shealladh i. "Calum an gaol orm? Chan eil e ach a' tarraing asam," thubhairt i, a' cur a-mach rithe fhèin.

Nuair a leugh e a' cheist a bha na sùilean, cha b' urrainn dha e fhèin a cheannsachadh na b' fhaide is ga tarraing gu bhroilleach, phòg e gu cruaidh i. Theann i ris, am mire na cridhe a' cur fuil theth a' ghaoil gu cruaidh tro a cuislean, is a' dubhadh às air ball gach allaban is ana-cothrom a dh'fhulaing i on a dh'fhàg i Alba. Bha a bith gu lèir a' seòladh air cuan sòlais, i taisgte gu tèarainte na ghàirdeanan, is a cridhe a' meathadh le dìoghras a phòige.

"M' eudail is m' ulaidh, Caitrìona bheag. Thusa de dh'uile mhnathan an t-saoghail don tug mise an gaol fallain, thoir dhomh do làmh is do ghealladh," thubhairt e, ga leigeil ma sgaoil.

Bha a bhriathran leatha mar ghaoith fhann, bhuig an t-samhraidh no mar chrònan an t-sàile is fhreagair i le a sùilean a' sileadh. "Seo dhuit mo làmh is mo ghealladh – an gealladh nach fannaich gu dìlinn gus an sìn mi sa bhàs." Thill i an sin gu a bhroilleach, a bilean a' sireadh a phòig is tacain bha i fo sheun le blàths a teò-ghaoil dha.

Nuair a thug iad a-mach an taigh-osda air achlaisean a chèile, rinn iad an inntinn an àird gun rachadh iad dhachaigh air a' chiad itealan. Is mun do dh'fhàg iad, gheall Calum gun cuireadh e fainne-gheallaidh air a meur nuair a ruigeadh iad Glaschu.

"Is an sin thèid sinn gu ruige Eisdeal," thubhairt i gu sunnd-ach.

"Mar as àill leat, eudail," fhreagair e.

An ùine ceithir làithean, bha a màthair a' cur fàilte chridheil orra an Eisdeal. As an sin, thog iad orra gu Beinn na Faogla far an robh iad air an èigheach. Is an ceann tri seachdainean – am fianais na sgìre – thug iad bòidean teann a' ghaoil.

An dèidh mìos nam pòg a chur seached san Eilean Dhubh, thill iad do dh'Eisdeal. B' ann an sin a thog Calum a' cheist a bha a' cur air on là san do phòs iad. "Feumaidh mi obair a lorg, thubhairt e. "Is cinnteach gum bi thusa a' dol air ais gu 'n dotaireachd?"

"Bithidh gu teagamh, ach chan ann an Albainn."

"Is càit' eile? Canada ma dh'fhaoite?" dh'fharraid e fo iongnadh.

"Chan ann, a ghaoil, ach an Afghanistan."

"Afghanistan, a luaidh! A bheil tu às do chiall gu buileach?" thubhairt e, a' chùis air dol sa mhuileann air.

"Chan eil idir, a ghràidh," thubhairt i an dà-rìribh. "Nuair a bha thu san taigh-òsda a-raoir, bha mi a' coimhead air prògram a rinn Sanndaidh Gall mu Afghanistan is a rèir na sgeòil tha am Mujahideen an cruaidh fheum air lighichean. Is cò aige tha fios nach bi dreuchd mar chomhairlich a' feitheamh air màidsear gleusda mar thu fhèin."

"Feumaidh mi aideachadh gu bheil thu làmhach, ladarna, eudail. Bha mi a riamh furasda mo thoirt a thaobh, is on nach eil ach leud ròineig fuilt eadar ciall agus cuthach, thèid mi leat." Is ga tarraing gu bhroilleach, fiamh gàire air aodann, thubhairt e, "Cha bu lugha na amadan a dhèanadh a leithid ach feumaidh na dh'fheumas on tha mise fo chuing leis a' ghaol."

Mar a tha an sean-fhacal Laidinn ag ràdh: 'Varium et mutabile semper faemina.' 'Tha am boireannach a-riamh is roimhe caochlaideach is aotrom an gnè.'

John Burnside

THE FARMER'S WIFE

I thought I knew him then:
that morning when he came
from lambing, white as a sheet,
and sat in the kitchen,
staring a hole in the table.
I waited him out,

and, later, he told me the story,
then told it again
to anyone come from the village,
wanting the loan of a book,
or a word of advice,

and always a piece of it missing,
that no one would guess:
the smell of the caul, that
mess spilling out on the floor.
It took several minutes
to die, and I think what he thought
he saw was the face of a child,
a father's likeness
clouded in its eyes.

I let that go.
But not what I know
he imagines, swerving away
from home and warmth
on winter afternoons
scanning the river,
watching for some return,

for he's learned the gaps
in vertebrae and stone
and stories where the dipper in the stream
is waiting to carry the soul
to the other side,

and when I see him
waiting in the dark
I can almost believe it is real, the way I once
imagined I could walk a road too far
and vanish
in the sound of my own breathing.

Gerry Cambridge

THE FIRST

Sue Richardson! She had what is called *it*.
Men buzzed like nervous bees when she was near.
Wordless, she electrified the atmosphere
in sea-green frock, as she would sit,
her legs demurely crossed, and sip hot coffee.

A neighbour. She was my introduction
to woman's mystery and dreamt seduction,
And I the light that couldn't escape her gravity.

My frame unfilled, a bumbling adolescent,
silk-minded, I hoped the marvel would occur
as I searched woods for nests – that I'd find her,
far from the smoky living room's covert looks.
There, her nearness charged my circuits incandescent.
And I plunged deeper into my nature books.

OBSESSION

The AA Book, of British Birds. I'd got
the Latin names of each of them by heart
at fifteen, and showing off would start
reciting. And I was proud knowing what
nidifugous, nidicolous, meant, in all weathers
tramping Cunninghamhead, delighted when I saw
verified, a dead heron's pectinated claw
one evening as I searched for eggs and feathers.

Oh neo-Wordsworth! Nidicolous youth!
Each May I could have told where a hundred nests were.
I knew where every summer migrant went.
Strix aluco I repeated, mantra for the truth.

Sue Richardson passed me in a swoon of scent.
I never found a Latin name for her.

Hugh Christie

BURGHEAD

aye
back in the seventies
he bought a thurd share in the 'Adonis'
when there wis money in mackerel
an faith in God ...
aye
early ane January
he wis due back
tae carry the Clavie
but 9 days oot fae the Winged Camp
– an that's fit they cried it
when the Romans seen this coast
in a hunner BC –
well Christ they musta hud
blistered hands
fightin thon swell ...
aye
an the wifie More
bidin hame wi er tea an stovies
yerds fae the hing she hated maist
an hearin its tides
a the time ...
aye
an mind er loons
baith the spit o im
an drammin efter the Kirk ...
well she kens far they'll awa tae
an if she needs salt fir the wounds
she'll ken far tae get it.

Ken Cockburn

SPINS AND TURNS

After the bells we'd had enough
of the country danceband's steady beat
and straightaway I found some jazz
that was nearer the mark; light, quick,
trying to catch itself out with spins and
turns dreamt up then and there.
I danced round the bed you lay on with
the end of the wine, that was nudging you
the other side of sleep
and you switched out the light, suggesting
I should switch off the radio too
but the music was suiting my mood, and besides,
then it stopped. The announcer announced
there was only time for one more number
and they'd do the 'Doctor Kildare' theme.
I knew you wouldn't mind too much.
So I sat at the foot of the bed you were falling
asleep in, almost, but not, in darkness,
light from lampposts and maybe the moon
seeping in through the curtains, and I listened
as they revived 'Doctor Kildare'
slowly becoming aware that
in front of me the lemon geranium
was oozing oxygen into
the atmosphere of the room, you know,
one of those meaningful insights that come
when you're half-asleep and half-pissed.
Applause. I switched the radio off
and joined you, gratefully, in bed.
Once I realised
I hadn't caught the band's name
I realised
I wasn't about to lose sleep over it.

Frances Corr

RAPID UNDERCURRENTS

You could tell when things had caught up on her again. The chair was piled high wi her gear and there wasn't any wholesome cooking going on. Rapid was her name. It was yon way when everything was bouncing balls at her and she didn't know quite how to return them. Rapid clapped eyes on hersel in the mirror. It was a laugh. The big jumper over the night shirt affair. The hot water bottle under her oxter. Millions o hair. Face as white as the proverbial shirt button. What's goin on at all, she thought to herself. Life's a bloody marathon. How come my phone keeps goin wi folk on the other end about to commit suicide. Christ.

And every night she had simple and amusing Dingly Dell sort of dreams but reality out there seemed to be darkening and closing in somewhat. She couldny make head nor tail of it. Aye Rapid could see the very evidence of the conflict in her very own home. She kept a tight rein on her living room and hoovered the corners and ordered offensive objects out with a straight arm and pointed finger. Neat. This was one room that had to have space and order. To lie down in and breath.

Over the threshold the turmoil faced her and caused the Scottish brow to knot. The kitchen was a struggle. A bunch of daffodils cheap at the price, 50p for two lots, stood erect and turgid in a big jar on the wiped table surface. Hmm blossoming. Managing to bloom yellow amongst the washing and stuck pots. Things could be worse, Rapid thought, as she moseyed past that doorway. There's a hell of a lot to do, she pondered, but with one sweep of my warrior arm I could clear a week of responsibilities and claim it as my own.

There was a continual succession of items in her geggy. A fag, a drink or six shortcake biscuits which were much smaller nowadays than they used to be. Still they were good and Scottish. Scottish butter and recipes caused pride to surge through her veins. There was something good and upright about that. Clan battles. Heather. Words like Culloden. She'd drawn thistles on the wall in biro while listening to another troubled voice on the phone delivering problems down the line. This was a time of change for Rapid. Her very outline was shimmering like electric.

Home was a tomb. Door double locked to keep the world at bay. Yet in a funny way it was where the world hit her most. The week's doings would follow her in the door like a swarm of bees before she could get turned round and the door shut. And it took a time for the buzzing to stop and the bees to settle before she could sit down and look at them and get to know them individually. Some of them she took to and some, well, she wasn't just terribly sure about. It wasn't in her nature but some just simply deserved to be splatted forthwith. Absolutely no doubt about it.

Bed was always good. There wasn't much she could think of at this particular point in her life to beat it. Absolutely unanimously each part of her body would collapse splayed on the firm flat clean surface. Here was no intrusion. Solitary peace. Bliss. Hallelujah. She crashed on to it like a collapsing building, and realising there was no hanky in the near vicinity she reached for her pyjama bottoms which lay by her pillow, and blew her nose on them copiously. She lit a fag and briefly stared cross eyed into the deep warm glow of the short flame from her red lighter – 50p from the Offy, a bargain for such a beautiful object, before dissolving into the tardis of her head.

Someone had informed her through the week that the ring round Saturn was actually made up of loads of rocks and chunks of ice hurtling round at high speed. She imagined tilting her head forward into that ring and how it would rummel about and be deafened by a noise like tatties in a tattie peeling machine. And how you could very simply bring your head back out again and all would be calm. Retreat. Her life was like this. She had control and the power to decide whether to be in it or out looking at it.

The deep and exciting thought was interrupted suddenly as she needed toilet badly. So she carried her global universal head through to the toilet aloft on her shoulders to partake in the very humble and irritating duties of dirrilling on a cold and harsh Scottish pan. She smiled in appreciation of her freedom to choose to re-enter the warmth of the bed and sit up with plenty pillows. Pillows gu-leòr. And return to that section of her brain that had warmed up nicely into displaying some promise in the way of entertaining thoughts. Better than Jonathon Ross, she thought. I only laughed once tonight in front of that telly. I'm glad I haven't paid my licence.

She thought an awful lot because she lived alone. There

was absolutely no reason why she should complain about her weeks because she liked what she did. She chose to be in the rush. She enjoyed to dip. That's what some boys call sex… A dip. She could relate to that. Dipping in and pulling out. It was addictive. The adrenaline rush of dipping into the Rapids. That's where she got her name. She also went rapidly through a packet of fags. Wow, she continued. The next thing you know this government will make you pay tax on entertaining thoughts. Or there'll be adverts for the Job Club coming up at regular 13 minute intervals in your head.

Rapid had a fine bunch of chums. But she couldny make head nor tail of them either. Christ it was mind blowing enough to be involved in her own head never mind anyone else's. From time to time all she wanted was a quiet life. Time to sit and hear the wind whistle up the lum.

Rapid was a cool name she thought. Better than being called Apple or something. It conjured up pictures of being a Red Indian in a waistcoat of animal hide with rough cut fringes. She liked turnips also. In fact she loved them with a passion. With their tough flesh and wise weathered skins, turnips captured the essence of the earth. Only this evening after Jonathon Ross she'd been playing with her large dictionary and came up with the word Napiform. It meant turnip shaped. She'd have endless fun with her dictionary, holding it to her heart and feeling it, then with closed eyes and meditative movement open it mystically and let her finger lead her to a point on the page. The eyes would open with the excitement of a child on Christmas morning to find a word that could give her more food for thought and meaning about her life than Justin Toper's horoscope line at 30p per minute. Tonight it was 'river-wall'. A wall confining a river within bounds. And she thought how apt. Especially with a name like Rapid. And this conflict carry on. The fight to keep order in the surging chaos. And the fight to keep blooming. But it's better than to lay down and die, she concluded. Or stagnate like a pond. Things could definitely be worse, she repeated to herself. I could've got a word like scab or rotten.

One night she'd done it with a chum who was black of mind. Whilst tippling to make merry of the situation as ever, her finger led her firstly to 'drinking' and secondly to 'excess'. On another occasion whilst desperately searching for enlightenment she landed on 'forefinger'. And proceeded to stare at her own in an effort to figure out this message. Perhaps it could've been leave the room along with the objectionable objects.

Terrible what boredom does to you, said her upstairs neighbour one morning as Rapid had zoomed down the stair. Her neighbour mopping vigorously in the close whilst making light of life. That's the spirit, thought Rapid.

It was quite something, considered Rapid, as she settled over on to her fleshy left hip, collecting her hotty around her stout ankles, how you could be so far into your own head but at the same time be aware of your neighbour below's chortles on a Saturday night. And trying to work out who's all in and what they've been up to. A whole tenement full of souls with ongoing thoughts no matter whether they be wiping a surface or drunk and oblivious in the corner of a crowded room. In fact a whole street full of thoughts and electrically charged brain cells with currents jumping like spark plugs. Fascinating. And when it comes down to it a whole region and o no a whole globe. At this point Rapid's head blew a gasket so she got up and made a homely pot of Earl Grey tea and arranged the tea cosy just so. This could be the cause of global warming she worried. Too much intense thought and not enough simple tasks like turnip howking.

She also had quite a good relationship with peanut butter. It was wholesome and good for you and it did when Rapid had a craving for peanuts and there weren't any. She remembered she'd seen it on Tomorrow's World that peanuts were good for your teeth. Rapid had re-settled in her scratcher parallel to a line of desirable objects alongside, between her mattress edge and the skirting. These consisted of an ambient yellow lamp with a napiform base, a stout and level headed sort of mug, the kind you'd put your trust in, and then a sociable green pub ashtray. The douts were tortured looking however. Smoked to the filter and screwed and twisted mercilessly as if they'd died a painful death at the hands of a nervous person. Neighbouring the ashtray was the now light box of fags and the very acceptable red lighter. A gold rimmed flowery plate, like that which would belong to an auntie, fought for a place on top of some books with the set of earphones whose cable led to the walkman containing one of many relaxation tapes. The largest piece took up end position as in a tug of war. The teapot with a bobble on top. Rapid's eyes had now grown weary. That bobble's stupit looking, she thought. Self doubt was setting in.

Fatigue was becoming evident inside her woolly cuffs and neck-line. She'd become abusive to her teapot. And viciously critical of her surroundings and world. I'll give you Dingly Dell, she thought. I'll give ye Dingly effin Dell.

And rightly so. The hours she'd put in trying to defend her territory like the Assynt crofters. Little wonder her face was grey with a line right across the forehead. Little wonder her hands were calloused and rough with wielding an axe at her doorway. Trying to preserve the space she'd fought for. Retain the oxygen therein in order for her plants to thrive. She had been known to spend hours beating her walls to chase the enemy away. And all the world could do was commit suicide on her.

Rapid went to sleep that night and left the world to continue attempting suicide. Meanwhile she floated off and revisited Dingy Dell where she was given a big blue stone, a rawhide waistcoat and a workspace.

When the morning stirred her creaking bones, she had a big grin on. Her eyes fell upon her bedside line of items. They were higglety pigglety now where she'd been in about them last night. The green ashtray heralding a glorious heap of poison, and the white daylight showing up the dust on her ambient lampshade. Reality fell on her and pushed her grin away. She humped through to the bathroom and ran both taps into the basin. I'll wash my hands of this, she thought. I'll wash my fuckin hands of this. And she took the bargain cake of soap at 4 for 30 odd pence and scrubbed and scrubbed and scrubbed. Then she strode through to the bedroom and flung her windies wide open and shouted out Over My Dead Body you'll commit suicide Over My Dead Body. Her frilly curtain blew gently in the wind as if to nod in solidarity. The bulbs were comin up well. It was a new day and it was hers.

Then up from the backs came a voice. Aye, it's terrible what boredom does tae ye eh? It was upstairs neighbour vigor-ously hingin oot the washin and making light of life. Rapid let out a bellow of laughter and thought to herself aye, that's the spirit, that's the fuckin spirit.

Jean Cooper

BEACHDAN EILE

Tha luchd-stiùiridh a'toirt seachad comhairle
do'n òigridh,
's iad ann o chionn linntean.
Tha iad inbheach, glic,
urramach nan dreuchdan,
ionnsaichte, làn eòlais.
Chan eil an saoghal caochlaideach
gam mealladh mar a bha e uair
's iad fhèin òg.
Tha iad ceart, 'nam beachd fhèin
's am fianais an t-sluaigh,
agus tha iad riaraichte.

Nach neònach seo matà;
Gun do choisinn thusa
cliù a thuirt iad
nach b'urrainn dhut,
agus na buaidhean
ris an robh iad an dùil,
cha d'rinn thu a'chùis orra
riamh.

'S fhuair thu dìteadh
airson sin.

OTHER OPINIONS

Guidance officers give advice
to the young,
as they have for generations.
They are of high status, wise,
honoured in their profession,
learned, experienced.
The changeable world does not
deceive them as it did once
when they were young themselves.
They are right, in their own view
and in public opinion,
and they are satisfied.

How strange then;
that you won
renown of which they said
you were incapable,
and the achievements
which they expected,
you never managed at all.

And you were condemned
for that.

MADAINN DI-LUAIN

Tha toll ann am mullach an trannsa,
ceàrnag fosgailte
ris an dorchadas,
aisnichean fiodha
is sgàilean gun chruth
rim faicinn,
's an t-uisge glas
ag èalaidh
gu oir na beàirn
's a'sileadh
air a shocair.
Boinneachan
seach ma seach
a'lasachadh an greime.
Plub!
      (Leig d'anail.)
Plub!   Plub!
'S iad a'tuiteam a-nuas
do'n ùrlar fhliuch.

Seachdainn 'sa chaidh
bha luchd-càraidh ann
's iad a'peantadh na callaid,
air eagal 's gun tig
fear-naidheachd an rathad
le camara
a'toirt am follais
bloigh meirg.

MONDAY MORNING

There is a hole in the corridor roof,
a square open
on the darkness,
wooden ribs
and formless shadows
visible,
and the grey water
creeping
to the edge of the gap
and dripping
gently.
Drops
one by one
loosening their grip.
Plop!
      (Take a breath.)
Plop!   Plop!
Falling down
to the wet floor.

Last week
there were repairers
painting the fence,
in case a
reporter comes by
with a camera
publicising
a speck of rust.

Robert Crawford

BABBY

Pirnie-taed babby,
Yir whorlbanes an trams,
Yir wee spyogs bane o ma bane,

Watchin *Dad's Army* wi yir knaps,
Ee me wi yir hailskint, unhattered skin
Kennin aathing that's yir ain.

Pirnie-taed	pigeon-toed
babby	baby
whorlbanes	hip-bones or joints
trams	(jocular) legs
spyogs	paws/hands/feet/legs
bane	bone
knaps	kneecaps
ee	eye
hailskint	having an unblemished skin
unhattered	without skin eruptions or sores
kennin	knowing

Penelope Daft

SNAKES AND LADDERS

Remand.
You start off at the bottom. Literally.

On the ground floor, you are not allowed to light your own fag. This is in case you torch yourself or the building. Instead you call through the hatch in your door – if it's open. If not, you sit silently, waiting for the sound of footsteps or rattling keys, then pound on the door with your hand and call out, trying to catch the screw's attention. If they are in a good mood, you get a light: if they've had a bad night, or are generally pissed off, they make you wait. You are ignored. You hear them passing, going away. If you call too much, you wait longer. It seems like hours. Sometimes you've got your fag lit and it goes out as soon as they've gone. You gaze in horrified disbelief at the thing, sucking frantically in an attempt to bring it back to life. Rollies *never* relight: the tobacco isn't packed hard enough. I've spent hours waiting for that little glowing tip, a lungful of acrid smoke. I've despised myself for wanting it, needing it. I developed a system of rolling a mass of fags in readiness; when I got one lit, I chain-smoked till I felt sick. It didn't put me off smoking. It made me obsessed with getting a light at every opportunity. I could never relax, day or night.

After three weeks of gradually moving off obs, I was transplanted to the floor above. Having established that I was not a closet pyromaniac, they now granted me the privilege of lighting my own fag. New problem. The shop had run out of matches. We weren't allowed gas lighters in case we sniffed them and I didn't have a petrol lighter. Since there were no hatches in the upstairs doors, I didn't even have the option of nabbing the wandering screw. I was told it would take five days for the shop to be restocked. One screw brought a couple of boxes. They didn't go far and she got a bollocking. The rest of them didn't give a toss. *I'll go mad*, I thought. To no-one in particular, I said I'd probably hang myself. Pure frustration, not a statement of intent. Bad move. They took me literally. I tried to explain but the decision had been made: I was not 'ready' for the responsibilities of life on the top floor. I had to

start again. Now an 'official' suicide risk, I had to comply with
the SS routine.

The posse escorted me to the ground floor. I went into the
cell; they waited in the doorway.
'Take your clothes off.'
My skin crawled. 'No.' My body was shaking violently. I
was not allowed to run or fight. I could not take part in my
own humiliation. Would not.

Silence.

I wondered if they'd all charge forward in a rush. My knees
threatened to buckle so I hung onto the bars at the window.
One particularly brutish individual decided to take charge.
Pushing herself forward through the huddle in the doorway,
she crowed, 'I'll take them off.' Brown eyes like pebbles behind
her glasses. God o god. I was hanging onto the bars. Her
passage was stopped by the screws closest to me. They moved
together and she was blocked. Her eyes flickered from one to
the other; she was still wanting to find a way through. I waited.
White knuckles, white bars. One of the blocking screws spoke.
'You'll go to Sierra and we will take your clothes off.'

Sierra.
The punishment block.
My stomach churned. I didn't know what it was like, I only
knew it was worse than this. Christ.
'I'm not taking off my clothes.'
My voice was low, shaking. I was trying desperately hard
to control the tremors by keeping myself rigid. It didn't work.
'Right. You're going to Sierra.'

They moved forward, amoeba-like, and surrounded me. I
was escorted into the frost outside. The ground felt hard under
my slippered feet. I moved automatically: nothing was said.
The faces around me were quite impassive. Their expressions
conveyed nothing of their thoughts or intentions. They looked
big. Pink and fat. Bulls. Moving mountains of flesh held up by
tree-trunk legs, uniformly blue, waving their arms as they
walked; me in the middle, arms folded tight around my body.
Holding out the cold, holding me in. My fingers clamped to the

spaces between my ribs, alternating fingers of flesh and bone.

In Sierra, I was taken into a back cell. They are sound-proofed, situated apart from the others. Sierra staff tagged onto the group marching down the corridor, their faces white masks. Shiny skin stretched tight, narrowed eyes, pinched nostrils and clenched jaws. They looked drugged, clones.

The cell has no window, no bed.

A raised concrete platform four inches high with a foam-filled plastic mattress and a blue nylon sleeping bag with a pillow sewn in. The pillow is brick hard. There is a heating vent in the wall on the far right, a few inches above the concrete platform but the room is cold. The recessed lights are on all the time, little squares of glaring brightness covering a large part of the ceiling. Too high to smash. There is a grey cardboard chanty in the corner, next to it, two paper cups of water. Nothing else. My body tells me I'm underground. I know I'm not. It just feels like that.

A male nurse appears behind five screws. He looks at me. They all look. The Sierra screws are in front.
'Strip.'
'No.'

My heart is going like the hammers of hell, body still shaking. Arms tight. I turn around. They are behind me. I sense movement. I keep my back to them. I do not resist. I do not fight. I say nothing.

My body is a deadweight: they have to manoeuvre my limbs like a shop mannequin. I am not taking part. They work in unison, rough, silent, practised. They force me down to my knees. I stare at the wall. My clothes are coming off. I won't help. Buttons undone, zip down. My body is a ragdoll. Knees in my back, hands gripping my shoulders, pinching me, pulling me, pushing me. I concentrate on nothingness. The wall. When I'm down to my underwear, they have to force me down, face down on the stone floor. My eyes are still open. Sore. I see the floor; pitted, painted concrete. I still won't help. Memories of rape. I am naked as a corpse. They pull me back onto my knees and the brown nylon strong dress is shoved over my head.

They do not pull it down. My arms are limp, hanging: I do not try to find the armholes. The dress hangs around my neck. It's very cold. The door slams behind me.

Involuntarily, I piss myself. I'm still kneeling. Urine, hot, pungent, collects round my knees, spreading across the floor. I crawl to squat with my back against the cold stone. The nylon dress slips of its own accord but is still only half-way down. It transfers cold. It doesn't warm up. My feet and hands are like ice, my toes and fingers very red. They hurt. Dried urine stings my legs. I won't think. I bang my head against the wall, harder and harder. My head doesn't crack, it bounces. The muscles in my neck ache as I throw my head back again and again. I don't want it to bounce. I want it to smash into a thousand tiny pieces, like the rest of me. I'm ashamed I can't hit it hard enough.

I get into a rhythm, steady as a heartbeat.
They keep coming to the door and telling me to stop.

My head buzzes. I've decided to die. I won't eat or drink. I'll just die.
They bring me food. No cutlery, more paper cups to scoop up the congealed mess on the plate. I piss in it, I piss everywhere but in the chanty. The floor is swimming. It looks like gallons and gallons. Liquid spreads. My piss, his blood.

I tear off a piece of the chanty and block up the spy-hole in the door. They've got another, higher on the wall. I didn't know it was there. I can hear scraping or a chair as they stand on it to look in. I try to hide in the corner. Too wet. The only dry bit left is the raised platform. I crawl into the sleeping bag and huddle closer to the vent. Nothing. No warm draught of air. I stay there just in case and pull the end of the sleeping bag tight over my head, away from eyes and light. It's cold. Dark and airless. I hope I'll suffocate.

There was no way of telling time.
Day and night were the same. Periodically, different people came to the cell. There was a nurse who wanted to check for bruising. I told her to fuck off.
'I'll just put down there's none then.'

'You do that.'
Then there was the doctor. I had my blood pressure taken.
Fuck off.
The psychiatrist came and went.
Fuck off.
They said I could smoke if I ate. I told them I'd given up.
FUCK OFF.
A voice called through the door. 'It's OK, I'm the night-nurse, a different shift. Do you want to talk?'
FUCK OFF.

Stinking, unwashed, I was finally put in front of the Sierra governor for my report. I was given a dressing gown and slippers and led to a chair. Two screws stood in front of me, an inch away but leaving a gap between them so I could see the governor but not attack. That's the procedure for every report.

My lips were dry and cracked. I could feel them splitting as I spoke. The remand screw spoke on my behalf. She said it had been a 'mistake', a 'misunderstanding'.
I was given a warning. They always give you something.

After dressing and cleaning the cell I was taken back to Remand. The ground floor. Mattress, sleeping bag, strong dress, cardboard chanty and a window. Only one screw.

But she had to make *sure* I wasn't wearing any pants under the strong dress.

Elspeth Davie

PROLOGUE TO THE NEW YEAR

1938–1939

Dec. 31st Friday
This will have to be a kind of Prologue to the New Year, written on its eve. As to the year passed there has been so much in
it that were it to go into the Prologue there would be no room
in this journal left for the story of 1938. There seemed somehow too much to express adequately and also not enough time,
but I have found now that somehow or other something must
be written with some regularity if only a few casual impres-
sionistic notes. I have not written with any regularity in the
past year, except, as a member of the student staff, to fill about
two pages every fortnight; but after a bit one feels almost a crying need to put something somewhere of all this amazingly
interesting business of living. This Prologue is perhaps more a
kind of prayer that I may be able to do justice to the business
with blue ink on a piece of white paper – an ambitious taste if
ever there was one but no less glorious if one manages to get
any kind of truth down whatsoever.

Bonnyrigg has the real 'Eve of something' stir about it tonight. Bessie, Lois and I were down in a vain attempt to get
chestnuts to roast round the fire, and found the place filled
with people bustling round with parcels, odd groups under
street lamps, dogs off the lead, children dancing around, probably thrilled with the promise of their staying up till midnight;
also the place seemed positively stiff with weddings – we've
already had two up here, confetti on the pavements, taxis
buzzing about at a great rate, bands of boys and girls out to
make whoopee somewhere. I suppose resolutions are in the air.
One of mine will have to be to write this thing with some kind
of regularity – another, to pull up my socks and try to keep
them from getting too absolutely indecently wrinkled next
year. Lately they seem positively to have been made of some
kind of special corrugated iron.

Certainly tremendous things have emerged from this year
not the least being Lois's engagement to Donald MacKinnon,
Moral Phil. tutor at Edinburgh and now Fellow of Keble
College, Oxford. At least it can be truly called an engagement

for those two are to all events pretty much 'fathoms deep'. He went up a few days ago but while he was here for a week he came out on a few occasions to supper. An extraordinary interesting person with definite sparks of something about him – genius perhaps, I don't know. A highly-strung sort of person with, especially on his first night here, all sorts of wild gestures and movements. When his mind was working full force on an argument he seemed to have no idea of what his body was doing. Large, rather ungainly, a beautiful voice, and now and then an extraordinarily tender expression when he smiled even in the midst of a rather heated argument. I gather he is a person with a bit of conscience, he is intense, certainly one of the most intense people I've met for a long time and, I think, will never find the world easy. I would say that they will both have times of being very happy and very unhappy which seems to me a better business than any long-drawn-out lukewarm state of affairs. He is an Anglo-Catholic and in that direction I suppose things will sometimes be a bit difficult for them both, but I think they'll come through all right. The main thing seems to be there.

The first term of my second 'varsity year has promised an interesting session. Philosophy and second English makes a lot of reading but it's great stuff. More of this later.

I suppose this goes under the conventional name of journal though what in the world that is may be some question to answer. A thing both subjective and objective, a mixture of ideas one's own and other people's on things worthy or unworthy, chance observations, things overheard and heard, seen and unseen – so let it be; we'll call it a journal. At any rate it's no time for apologies. This is a Prologue not an apology and as such I believe merits a few trumpet flourishes to raise the curtain on the various acts of the play. Well, here goes! And may it go well.

1938

Jan. 2nd Sunday
Daddy and I danced out the old year in an amazingly sudden unexpected way. At about eleven we set off to the Church Halls to have a look in at the second wedding party, but the affair was just about through, people still drifting about in rather a sleepy fashion, the bride standing in her wedding dress

looking rather dazed but also rather radiant, and her husband, white-buttonholed standing by. We danced a few dances, got our bag of wedding cake and stole out again. As we were passing the Masonic Hall we hear the sounds of some affair seemingly more gay and going lustily though it was close on midnight. The notice informs us that this is the Y.A.U. Hogmanay Dance 9–2, so in we step without further ado. At once we are plunged into a terrific scrum of people up on the floor, a smashing jazz band and a good many strange faces though there were a few I recognised. What we were doing there I don't think we ever quite found out, but when we at length emerged at half past one we had had a good many dances, an ice each and a definite shake up. I rather enjoyed it, coming as it did after a long day's feeling of deadness. I liked my almost indecently snappy dance with a simple looking soul who was all in his legs and feet, so to speak. I liked meeting a few people whom I have seen before only in certain definite settings and who have never seen either Daddy or myself at such a dance. I liked my ice and half an apple cake with Mr Moncrieff up in a funny loft-like place above the hall. I enjoyed meeting a little girl Jenny Harper and winning her from a rather defensive silence to a sudden friendliness in which she glowed with something very near prettiness, dancing the Spanish Waltz with Mr Moncrieff, Daddy and myself, I enjoyed this sudden plunge into the whole show and strangely, felt like it that night. Today and Saturday have been quiet days, mostly filled with reading, practising music, silent days but somehow not peaceful.

Jan. 10th Monday
Writing this up in the Fine Art Library – a most delightful place – beautifully lit and at this hour, quarter to five, very quiet. I come here for an hour's peace before a visit to Miss Mitchell and then a concert at 8. Rather a feeling of freedom to-day, having got the Social and International week's article off my chest, my music lesson over. Tomorrow 'varsity begins again, rather a good thing in a way and fine to tackle some good reading again. This holiday has been anything but peaceful especially before New Year and there has been little time to get all the reading and writing done, to say nothing of more peaceful days, long sleeps and walks on the hills which fill the imagination in the last week of term and cheat one into the belief of their possibility.

On Friday evening Daddy and I went as partners to the large Masonic Hall dance in aid of some children's affair. A very long business it was – from 9–4 but it was rather good fun. Lois went with Blythe Hume and most certainly they made a handsome couple. Eventually we joined their party which was made up of a good many young couples and dances with a good many different people.

Somehow or other I really felt like a dance that night – it makes a difference when there are good dancers and a band. Evidently the moving of the legs to a rhythm crooned or crashed out by a few drums and cymbals along with some delicate but nondescript trickles from the piano, a twang or two from a banjo, evidently this and a partner who can sway a bit and slip with some grace along a floor, may be a pleasure – a rum thought. There is a rather more unique pleasure in dancing with some of those lads who have brought their girls along – a happiness and a freedom which is not always felt when dancing with a person who is, as it were, footloose and fancy free because then, paradoxically, he may not feel nor his partner half so footloose and fancy free.

Adam Letham and his girl were there. Adam with an honest bloom in his cheeks which would have been the envy of any painted woman of fashion. A cabaret followed supper – good in bits – an extraordinarily clever conjurer doing impossible things with a fine air of confidence, deftly moving his hands while speaking calmly and reassuringly the while. He finishes a remarkable trick holding up his object or objects neatly in his finger tips, gazing round his audience, eyebrows raised in a quiet kind of triumph which seems to deny any explanation of the trick being raised. A tap-dancer also came on at intervals – a girl dressed in white evening jacket and trousers. The dancing has got a fascination because of the rhythm and a certain casual mechanic easiness about it, but it is most certainly not beautiful and when combined with a dance song which seems designed to express what is called love in about the most ungraceful metaphors that could be found (The Love bug will bite you if you don't look out), then it can only be called ugly. Left at about three, leaving L. still dancing. I read a few pages of Mary Webb's 'Precious Bane' in bed, a strange and lovely contrast to the evening.

Jan. 12th Tuesday

Miss Mitchell not being in last night I went to the concert myself after half an hour's reading in E.P.L. Met Joan Berry at the Usher Hall so we went in together. A very fine concert it was. Certainly even the stress of hard work and impossibly full and tiring days isn't a sound excuse for missing the possibility of the joy of such an evening's music. The programme consisted of three pieces – an Overture by Verdi, a concerto by Tchaikovsky played by Simon Barer, and a new symphony by Walton. All of these were most lovely. One phrase is remembered above all in the concerto played by them, consisting of only a few clear and cool notes but with a peculiar little lilt at the end, finishing on a note which gives the whole phrase the tone of a person saying something which leaves one wondering whether it was a compliment or if there wasn't a touch of irony in the voice. I was going to say at first that it had rather a questioning tone but no – for it was not exactly a lilt lifting one up but bringing one down gently on one unexpected note. I see now what is the difference between such a conductor as Szell and Barbirolli. The latter is quite a fascinating sort of person, his cuffs shoot in and out, he dances around a lot, sweeps back his hair, and conducts some sorts of things energetically and well, but he is not part of his orchestra; he somehow gets in between his audience and the orchestra which is his background. The other is one with the players, he has fine control and is master of the situation, never waving his arms around aimlessly or standing out in way from his orchestra. It is rather wonderful how, in a great piece of music, everything seems to be one with it, more especially when it rises suddenly to a terrifically excited tumultuous part. Even the player hurriedly tightening his drums and the trombone players shaking out their instruments, the conductor swaying in his stand – these become one. Do even the audience in their tense silence also become one with it? I was trying to see this, but somehow couldn't quite.

Perhaps they don't; are not yet sensitive enough as one mass of people to be fused into it. The various movements of the pianist and also the conductor are interesting in their variety. The pianist sits crouched almost fiercely over his piano, his hands jerking along the keys in a vibrant, almost harsh movement; the music dies into place and he relaxes a little, his fingers caressing, stroking the keys, moving smooth as flowers on water up and down, winning all the tenderness, the gentleness from these same keys which a moment before responded angrily, the notes springing up fiercely to his touch. The conductor also has as many movements as a dancer; he sways with the music, he dances, he jerks, nods, bows, beckons winningly to them and then lashes them into fury as though his baton were a whip.

Interesting it was to see Joan again. She is old and rather precocious for her age – sixteen. Strange to speak to her in the interval – she leaning against the wall, smoking, a pale rather proud face, young really, yet striving to be born into maturity, her two little strands of red pigtail hidden beneath her coat collar. With some people that is an age in which they strive in great pain to be born into maturity. Watching this one remembers and understands. A wonderful night it was, frosty and star-lit.

Today was first day of term. A rather remarkable one for me it was too. I've got a Bible-class social very shortly, to my sorrow but I'd like to get something written on today. In the first place I discover to my stunned amazement that I'd got 108 out of 200 for Phil., only to be congratulated later by Sister Aloisia in English on being second. Whether this be true or not remains to be seen, but the mark itself comes as the most astounding surprise.

I believe our lecturers for this term are Mr Sinclair and Porteous. Today we had Sinclair lecturing on the Nature of Knowledge which promises to be very interesting. There's something wonderfully reassuring about this young man, his voice, manner of speaking, expression – definitely one of the comforts of life.

In English this term, for 18th C. Prose, we have Dr Clark. I can think of few people so utterly different as Dr Clark and Dr Kitchen and the contrast of personality and lecturing is itself enough to make an interesting year.

Jan. 15th Saturday

A mighty wind tonight. L. and I were out fairly early before tea when it was not so strong, and the clouds were like great golden fishes against the pale evening sky. But later in the evening when we were out again the wind made one mad and terribly alive. Even to sit in front of the fire and listen to it was to become more and more restless to be out fighting with it and knowing its strength.

This time it was wonderfully clear, a full white moon and stars. Now the clouds were like long silver fish against the dark sky. More than ever tonight there is the sense of this living as a great race against Time and Eternity with the 'wingèd chariots' close at one's back.

Especially this last year I have had this sense of living against time, gasping against a great wind. Yet it is often a fallacy to call this immense struggle to keep one's head above water in so many things, living. The days when we truly live are days far more full of peace, more simple than this.

But the struggle against the wind was tremendously refreshing. Having sung against it, shouted against it, run against it, defeated it and been defeated by it, one could, at last, settle with a kind of peace by the fire again.

I have started Bertrand Russell's book of [essays] and find it very interesting. Have been reading also H. Bates' 'Fallow Land' and found it good. It is good to get back to some books about the country and country people after so many of subtle society tangles in town life. There is a melodrama here; it is simple with a kind of beauty of description which as in Mary Webb hardly surprises with its loveliness because it is so absolutely fitting in metaphor, and style to the whole atmosphere of the places described.

This from 'Precious Bane':

'There was but little sky to see there, saving that which was reflected in the mere; but the sky that is in the mere is not the proper heavens. You see it in a glass darkly, and the long shadows of rushes go thin and sharp across the sliding stars, and even the sun and moon might be put down there, for, times, the moon would get lost in lily leaves, and, times, a heron might stand before the sun.'

Jan. 18th Tuesday

I've got one of my terrible spasms of restlessness tonight which seems to come whenever I realise how much there is to be done, how much on top of me. And so I sit with books all around and can do nothing but rise up every little while to wander around, go downstairs for an apple or for no other reason than to go into another room for a bit; I try to play the pianola which is a no less wretched business, there being a squeak that fairly breaks the heart in the pedals. Even the beloved Bach and the perfect chord ending to Fantasia in A is spoilt.

Today I got back my second Phil. essay, Drever promised me B++ for it. He was rather encouraging, said that it was good, very interesting and the best that he'd got so far. After he'd criticised it and said a good deal he sat back and said, 'Now you're to do the speaking, any questions arising from your reading or from the lectures – anything.' I sat on the very edge of the chair and gaping into that roaring fire, completely mute, like a perfectly inadequate ass. After a bit I incoherently muttered something about Locke's primary qualities theory, which he went into at good length, I listened to no word. I can't think why I should go so ridiculously unprepared for questions especially when I know that individual tutorials, if made proper use of, are some of the best things in 'Varsity.

Our two committees yesterday were interesting ones, at least the last was. Between them Horace Walker, Jean T. and I went to a little restaurant for something to eat, then back to Jean's digs for the next committee. Really got down to things by the end. 10.20 bus home. Horace is an interesting lad; it's good to see him after so long. He can be the greatest fun so as to make you almost forget his seriousness and then perhaps suddenly in the middle of some flippant thing you're speaking about he'll become as serious as a judge, look completely indifferent to what you're saying, stare at the tablecloth, mutter 'yes' to what you're saying, and with a disconcerting abruptness leave you feeling absolutely in the air or at sea, if you like.

Jean is a most loveable person; one feels grateful to her grace in doing things, even quite little things, dealing with awkward people, awkward situations, smoothing all over with a gentle hand and yet absolutely alive to new things and ideas.

A week has gone by and I've very little work done. Must try to get a deeper sense of peace. I think I can never be happy unless doing some definite bit of writing, but there's so little time just now.

Angus Dunn

THE BEEKEEPER'S FACE

I became aware of a buzzing noise in the air. I stopped digging. In summer there's a constant hum of insect life around the garden, but this was far too loud. It might be a motor of some sort, but there was no-one nearby as far as I could see. The garden was empty, and the path was clear all the way up to the big house. Over the fence, the field was also empty, except for a dozen hives, far off.

I headed towards the orchard. The sound grew louder, but it was difficult to locate exactly. There are always bees around the fruit trees and bushes, but it was too loud for bees. I walked under the old apple tree, at the corner by the fence. The sound was louder here. I turned and bent down, scanning the ground to see what might be causing the noise. An insect landed on my neck. I brushed it off. There was nothing on the ground.

The sound seemed to be coming from the tree. The tree was old and gnarled, with cankers and rounded growths at the branchings. One of the cankers, on a branch just in front of me, seemed to be different in some way. The texture of the bark looked odd and it wasn't quite the same brown as the rest of the tree. A bee flew down and landed on it. The bee disappeared.

I looked closer: the entire surface of the growth was moving. There was an unpleasant crawling sensation in the small hairs on the back of my neck. Even before I realised why, I was running at full speed across the garden, frantically shaking my head in case any of the bees in the swarm had caught in my hair. Long after I was sure that there were no bees on me I could still feel them crawling on the back of my neck.

Ian Ross comes to take the swarm. He is very old. He comes down the steep track to the garden as fast as he can, leaning on his grandson's arm. He has no equipment, but his grandson is carrying a cardboard box.

'Where is it? Let me see.' His eyes are bright, excited.

I lead him through the gate to the orchard and point to the old tree.

He hobbles forward. Donny seems less eager, and the old man lets go of his arm.

I watch, near the fence, ready to run. Ian keeps reassuring his grandson. 'Don't worry. They don't sting when they're swarming.'

Donny is unsure. He stands a few feet back from the tree, holding the equipment at arm's length. 'It's easy for you to say that. You're not allergic to bee stings.'

I think I should keep Donny talking, to distract him. 'Allergic? What happens if you get stung?'

'I got stung once on the arm and it swelled up like a football.'

Ian is leaning close, looking at the swarm. He grunts. 'It's a good one. I'll need to feed it through the winter though. Give me the box.'

Donny hands him the box. Ian folds the flaps back, pulls out an old sheet and throws it to one side. The box is now empty. He puts it on the ground, directly beneath the swarm. 'Find me a stick.'

I find him a stick. The old man's eagerness is infectious. I step forward confidently, give it to him, then stand beside Donny. Ian begins to scrape the bees off the tree, tapping the stick each time on the edge of the box so the bees drop off. Some of them begin to fly around, buzzing loudly. One of them lands on the old man's hand, and I can see it stinging him.

Donny is getting jumpy. 'Did that bee sting you?'

'No,' the old man lies. He brushes the bee from the back of his hand. Bees are flying close around me now. I am afraid, but the fear is more like excitement: the old man is working the bees and he is not concerned. I watch him. I have rarely seen anyone so confident, so intent. His mind on nothing but the bees. I trust him. Donny is edging away. I take a step closer to the tree, watching.

Ian continues scraping bees off. There is a swirling cloud of bees around us now and the buzz is louder.

'Tchah!' A bee has got him in the side of the neck. He brushes it off.

'I'm going,' says Donny.

'It's all right,' says his grandfather.

A bee lands on my upper arm, where the T-shirt sleeve stops. It stings. I am not so stoical as the old man. 'Yow!'

Donny runs. I brush the bee off.

'Find a bigger stick.'

I find one.

'What are you going to do now?'

'The queen won't move. That's why the bees won't stay in the box. I'm going to dislodge her.'

He raises the stick above his head, and before I have time to work out what he's doing, he brings it down full force on the branch, beside the swarm. The swarm shudders. He thwacks the branch again. The brown crawling lump of bees falls into the box and bursts. I am over the fence and away while the first of the bees is barely in the air.

When I reach the tree where Donny is standing, I turn and look. Ian is hobbling determinedly away from the tree, using the stick to keep his balance.

He has to go round by the gate, and he is panting by the time he reaches us.

'That did it,' he says. 'They'll not move out of that box tonight.' He sounds pleased.

'You're going to leave the box there?' I ask.

'Just overnight. You'll need to put the sheet over them later, once they've all settled. Can you do that, or will I send Donny down to see to it?'

Donny doesn't look happy.

'I can do it,' I say. Donny looks relieved.

'I'll send Donny down in the morning with the van. He can bring them up to the croft.'

'Granda…'

'It'll be all right. Just wrap the sheet round them so they can't get out.'

In the morning Donny comes for the bees. He asks me to carry them up to the vehicle. With the bees safely in the back, he drives very carefully up the hill to the croft. He parks the van near the house and leaves the bees where they are.

'Tell him he can move them himself. I'm off.' Donny disappears down the hill.

In the croft house, Ian is beaming in his easy chair. His wife brings me a cup of tea. She doesn't look pleased. But she never does. I don't know if she can smile. I've never seen her try.

When she goes back through to the kitchen Ian gives me twenty pounds and winks at me. 'That's for telling me about the bees. Now don't you be saying a word about this to anyone. Jim Ferguson has big lugs.'

'Jim Ferguson? What's it to do with him?'

'He keeps the hives down at the field there. Did you not

know? It's a swarm off his hives.'

'Oh. Should I have told him?'

'No, no. You don't want anything to do with him. He's a bad old bugger.' He looks at me sharply, wanting to know my opinion of Ferguson before he says anything else.

I shrug. 'I don't know him that well.'

'Well, I've known him since he was too short to shite in a bucket. He wasn't too bad though, when he was young. I would take a drink with him, then.'

He sits quiet for a while.

'He's got a lot of hives down there,' I say. 'In the field. I've seen his honey in the shops too. He's doing well.'

Ian glares at me. 'That man knows nothing about bees that I never told him, but he's grown to have a very high opinion of himself. Bee stings don't bother him you see, not more than a pinprick.'

'That would be handy,' I say. 'For a beekeeper.'

Ian leans forward. 'There was a time Alecky and me and Ferguson were taking a hive of bees up to Lairg. The hive was covered by a sheet on the back seat, and Ferguson was sitting beside it, to keep it steady.

'At Loch Shin a big tourist car came round a bend without slowing and we didn't have time to find a passing place. We went off the road and into the ditch. The hive came off the back seat and the bees came roaring out.

'Me and Alecky jumped out of the car and ran for it. I wish I could still run like that. Anyway, fifty yards away we slowed down and looked back. Ferguson was watching us from the back window. The inside of the car was black with bees and he was roaring with laughter.

'He lifted the hive back onto the seat and walked over to stand with us. He'd even thought to take the sheet right off the hive.

'We stood there smoking and waiting for the bees to settle into the hive. Ferguson never said a word, but now and again he'd look sideways at Alecky and me and he'd have a laugh.'

Ian sits quiet for a while.

'Aye,' he says, 'he's good with bees right enough.' He looks at me sharply. 'But mean as a weasel. He wouldn't have given you a penny for that swarm, and he'd let them die in the winter, like as not.'

'Just like yours did, winter before last,' says his wife, from

the kitchen door.
'Aye, well it was a bad winter. Jim Ferguson lost some too.'
'He didn't lose all of them though.'
'No, I was unlucky there, right enough.'
There is an atmosphere growing in the house.
'Well I'd better be going.' I finish off my tea.
'I'll see you to the door.' He struggles in the chair. I hold my
hand up.
'No, Ian. Stay where you are.'
'I'll see him out,' his wife says.
At the door, she stands stiffly. 'Well, that's it. I don't expect
they'll swarm again.'
I grin. 'We might be lucky.'
She humphs as I turn to leave.

The fine weather continues. The bees swarm again. Ian
comes hobbling down to the garden again, looking a bit grey,
but burbling with excitement. I have to help him down the hill.
'Another one! Give me a hand, will you? Donny is away at
the shearing in Rosehall.' I help him to gather the swarm, getting stung again.
'Can you bring it up for me? I'll have a wee something for
you if you do.'
I don't want his money, but I'm happy to take the bees up
in the boot of my car, though I let him lift them out at the croft.
He shows me the hive with the first swarm in it. It's old, but
it seems to be sound. A few bees are moving in and out through
the door. There's another hive beside it. The wood is split and
the felt on the roof is torn.
'Lift the lid off for me.'
I lift the roof and look inside. It's dusty, and damp in one
corner.
'Let me at it.'
I move aside. Ian bends back the flaps of the cardboard box
then picks it up and pours it into the hive. He bangs the box a
couple of times with his stick then turns to me for the lid. I pass
it over and retreat a few yards. The bees are not happy.
Once the lid is on, he puts a piece of slate over the door.
'Best to keep them in till they're used to the new home.'
He comes over to stand beside me. Suddenly he looks tired.
Or maybe I've just noticed.
I take his arm. 'Come on. You'd best get inside.'

He doesn't argue. I help him into the house and into his chair in front of the TV.

Mrs Ross watches me from the kitchen door, her mouth pursed. With Ian settled, I have to pass through the kitchen to leave. Mrs Ross seems to be in my way.

'You'll take a cup of tea,' she says. It doesn't sound like a question. I sit down at the table.

She fills the teapot, sets one cup on the table and pours. She shuts the door through to the living room and stands across the table from me, arms folded.

'If there's another swarm, you'll not tell Ian.'

I want to ask why, but she's such a grim old besom that I sit quiet. It feels like I'm being told off.

She looks at me.

'You saw him with those bees. Jumping about like a child. At his age.'

I smile. 'He's a character all right.'

'He wouldn't be half such a character if you lot didn't encourage him!' She closes her lips tightly and glares at me. 'Can you not see he's acting up to you. Fifty years ago he could behave like a daft bairn and survive it. But half the damn fools in the Strath are taken in. They encourage him. And he's still acting the fool, though it's past his time.'

I don't know what to say. The tea's in front of me but I can't drink it. And I somehow can't leave without drinking it. It's keeping me in the kitchen while she has her say.

Her gaze doesn't waver. 'And what'll happen to those bees now?'

I shrug.

'They'll die. Stealing the bees off Ferguson – that was an adventure – and he had an audience for that. Looking after them through the winter? I'm the only one who'll see that, so he'll not bother, though he knows fine what needs done. The bees will die and he'll blame it on the weather.'

She is staring at me, silently. I pick up the cup of tea and stand.

'Thank you for the tea, Mrs Ross.' I walk past her and set the cup on the draining board.   .

She is still staring across the table at my chair.

'I'd better go now.' I turn to say goodbye at the door.

She stirs and looks at me.

'Well, I suppose it's no more your fault than anyone else's.

But if there's another swarm, don't tell him.'

'You think I should tell Mr Ferguson?'

'Anyone you like. But not Ian. He's got two swarms now that'll probably not last the winter.' She pauses and looks at me. 'And he's eighty-five years old. I don't know if he could take the excitement of stealing another swarm off Ferguson.'

Late in July, there is another swarm.

I call Ferguson.

'It's not a big swarm, I suppose,' he asks.

'Not very big.'

'It'll maybe just be a cast, at this time of year. I'll send a couple of the boys out to look at it.'

The boys never turn up. In a day or two the swarm finds itself a better home and disappears.

I don't see Ian again until the Spring. He doesn't mention the bees, and I don't ask.

Julie Ann Fullarton

BAD NEWS

Bad news (from the wishing well) of
Mysterious footsteps came by the wrong path,
Carried by a robin singing a fat song.
News of sparkling money and rushing water
Came down worn ways, to drop a black
Glove on the step of Gretel's house.

The stone face wept moss to hear the words.
The wee trees felt stripped of their character.
Gretel shook crumbs of her life from stiff skirts.
She locked the door of the gingerbread house.
She slipped the cold key inside the black glove.
Iced words grumbled and fidgeted.

'Hush' whispered Gretel as she stepped over
And was swallowed by the smoke.

The robin, sick with sorrow,
Bright as blood
Tapped on the sugar pane.

Robin Fulton

I GIVE BACK SOME BRIGHTNESS

Summer is a present tense.
I am snagged by my decades.

One more weight has been added.
It's invisible. The sun

stares at the almost-weightless
and the never-to-be-budged

and both oblige with brightness.
My present tense tries to be

translucent as a thin leaf
and opaque as a thick stone

both at once. I give back some
brightness. And hide away some.

A spider's web makes the best
of two worlds, half-hanging on

to earth, parachuting on
its fistful of half-held air.

LARGE QUESTIONS

Such as time, and light. The afternoon plays
thirty-two variations per minute
on pewter-grey. White pain spills from nowhere
and bounces off the incorrigibly
unsettled sea. A man sits among rocks
with paint-tubes. His brush seems to be manic
rubbing rubbing at a stain that won't give.

We're drawn to the edge of land expecting
and finding largeness, hesitant margins
where chroniclers definitively set
'Here began', 'Here flourished' and 'Here ended'.
Marram-grass roots defy shouldering dunes
bring them to a standstill. Nervous-headed
harebells, unlikely survivors, survive.

Tomorrow fills the space of yesterday.
The painter has brought home a small answer
a rectangle, a mirror, a blind-spot.
The uncertain harebell is now immense
in memory, overwhelming today.
A question has been asked, too small for words.
An answer has appeared, too large for words.

The paint has stopped moving. No-one can say
if the harebell is nodding or shaking.

Donald Farquhar

THE DAFT STANE

The stane kent it wis the warld's pin
as the mune keekit here an there.
The stane stude, its face tae the waa
the warld birled on by itsel.
The birks drapit blades on the stane's heid
as the rain washed its gray face.
Whiles the wund kaimed the stane's pow
an the stane kent it wis the warld's pin.

The stane kent it wis the warld's pin.
Syne the mune luikit doun, leerie like
pouin the watters ahint it.
Bit the stane stude its grun
as the seas faem kittled aroun its taes
an the warld birled on roun the sin.

Paul Finn

THE BODYGUARD'S REVOLVER

beneath chestnuts and poplars
only Lyonnet could understand the complex Loire
from Nantes to Nevers
hearing what you had already said
a choice is chosen
the soul prevails but does not aspire:
a shape of sorts – chance, misfortune?
you prefer to die in Nevers;
rich in those alluvial soils
along the well-tramped towpath
of the Canal de la Jonction
for two hundred metres or so
Saturday evening anglers and lovers
it was spring
far from the 'château'
a small clearing
stolen from the glove compartment
and in your hands
the bodyguard's revolver.

Pete Fortune

WAVING AT STRANGERS IN PASSING CARS

The Ancestral Home
6th June

Dear Meg

Thank you for your letter(s). Still seems strange receiving them without the accompanying rejection slip. Glad you liked the photograph by the way, and no, I don't think I do look like him.

In reply to another of your questions: I don't know if it was Philip Roth or not who wrote 'Patrimony – A True Story', and no, I haven't read it, nor do I think I want to. Besides, it can't have been **that** good if you're not even sure who wrote it! Are you suggesting I write my own version? As for what you have to say about my existing writing:

'If your stories are read as a transcript of a general mood – and I've made a point of reading everything I could lay my hands on – then things with you always seem pretty bleak. But isn't it easier to write that way – i.e. more natural – because of a lot of the things going on in the world today? Maybe not just today? The ratio of OH MY GOD *stories to* YIPPEE *ones always has been pretty high. I often ask myself why that should be the case. Any thoughts on the matter yourself?'*

Sorry Meg, but I haven't a clue. If I do have a sneaking sus-picion as to why, then I'm afraid I lack the necessary energy to explore it in any depth. But listen, it's maybe as simple as this – happy/contented folk are too busy getting on with their lives to waste it sat in front of a keyboard inventing imaginary lives. They leave that to all the miserable sods who are without friends or social life.

And the business of writing and getting it all wrong simply adds to the misery. The most poignant piece I ever wrote was the *Gregor Cooper* story, about the big booze fiend dropping dead in the off-licence and the proprietor's total inability to deal with the situation, emotionally I mean. I was totally drained after writing that piece. I wrote it in one sitting, was simply compelled to keep at it until finally I collapsed into bed around 5am. I felt exhilarated though, was convinced I'd unearthed something both beautiful and profound anent this booze fiend dropping dead. It was almost as if I'd canonised him. Meg, people tell me it's the most hilarious thing I've ever written.

Oh jolly fucking ha ha. Big guy's just snuffed it and poor old Gregor's astride his chest, trying to pump life back into that body and worrying all the time that he might cave the guy's ribs in. Then the ambulance people arrive and as far as they're concerned it's no big deal. Sniggering about it being quite a place for an alcoholic to breath his last, they cart the dead body off as if it was just a lump of meat. Poor Gregor is left abandoned and practically removed from his senses. Eventually he puts a little sign up on the shop door which says CLOSED DUE TO BEREAVEMENT and then he wanders the streets in a daze, convinced that he and everyone he loves are about to snuff it because the big booze fiend just proved how effortless the whole business really is. Oh jolly fucking ha ha.

If that was the most poignant thing I've ever written then one of the most poignant things I've ever witnessed was when we were taking a walk in the countryside one Sunday afternoon. A good two miles from home my son, who was three years old at the time, was consumed by the urgent need to take a shit. We duly hid him behind a dry-stane dyke where he proceeded to drop an almighty dollop. Later, after a very silent journey home he turned to me and asked, 'You won't tell my friends, will you?'

That Meg, would serve well as my motto, if not my epitaph. If you detect an overwhelming sense of despair in my work, then please keep it to yourself. You won't tell my friends, will you?

All my friends go away. One went to the States to become a barman and get shot at (occupational hazard he says), an old lady friend finished up mad as a brush (beware the consequences of continuing this correspondence – you may end up as a nut Meg) and my next door neighbour friend committed suicide in his garage. His house is up for sale now and I'm a keyholder, and am expected to show prospective buyers round the place. I told the people at the solicitor's office that I didn't mind doing this. And nor do I mind doing this, but raising his garage door one particularly dark wet and windy evening, a young couple asked what had become of the previous owner. Just for the sheer hell of it I told them, and suggested that if they took possession of the place they keep that fact to themselves.

In short, not to tell their friends.

You run out of friends the older you get. Heed this Meg – our old dad always said the only real friend he had was my mother. I was never sure whether he intended this as a complaint or to demonstrate what a sound marriage they had. Sometimes if he said this loudly enough she would wheesh him because she couldn't hear the telly. Anyway, it wasn't true because he did have friends, albeit what seemed an odd assortment for him.

When I was a wee boy, as well as having a daytime job our dad worked of an evening as a barman, in the local Tory club. Imagine it! He was an old communist of sorts (he certainly believed in sharing everything) and to eke out his miserable pay he'd to take an evening job pouring pints and G+Ts for the local Tory crew. Some of them used to give him a lift home at closing time and come in for a drink or ten. Occasionally a mob of them would appear, cars coming and going all night it seemed. But that's all it was. I was just a wee boy and it just *seemed* that way. Probably they were all gone by midnight. I didn't get to see much of them but I heard them often enough. I used to lie awake wondering at all that drunken din and then peer out the window and wave at them when my mother had decided enough was enough.

My mother was always in her dressing gown when the Tories dropped by. One Saturday morning up the town we encountered one of them, a half mad German. This half mad German spotted my mum and outside *Woolworths* he roared JESUS CHRIST WOMAN I NO RECOGNISE YOU AT FIRST WITH YOUR CLOTHES ON.

She told him to wheesh too.

But yes our dad had friends but for some reason tended to deny that. Maybe he really hated their guts but had to go through the motions simply to keep himself in evening employment? I doubt if that was the case actually. They used to argue like mad about politics and he wouldn't have done that if he had felt in any way intimidated by them.

Listen.

What would the chat have been like if he'd worked in some ordinary old boozer? What chance then a lift home from wealthy men armed with bottles of Scotch? Old commie or not, he knew what he was about. I realise now there was more to our dad than meets the eye.

He went to the club not realising he still had his slippers on one night, and he used to talk about that a lot too. That and how mum was his only real friend. He would bring the slippers story up every so often and I would pretend I'd never heard it before. It became a kind of legend in the club and eventually old Jake Lockhart brought a pair of *his* slippers into the club and would wear them whenever he felt like it. Dad said that in no time at all the place was all cluttered up with slippers. He said too that he was expecting the pyjamas and the dressing gowns to appear any time.

He wasn't likely to stray too far with his slippers on, eh? Nor were the others. Jake Lockhart and mad Herman. Ted McCabe the golfer and the old guy who was the photographer with the *Standard*. These were our dad's friends, Meg.

Or at least acquaintances. If my kids see me talking to someone in the street they automatically assume it is a friend. Kids are always automatically assuming, which is why they have little sense of danger at times. But *my* kids. My kids have loads of friends, hundreds of them. Come birthday party time the *Wimpy* is simply over-run with them and doesn't my wallet know it! But the years will pick them off, peel them away like dead skin. They've probably still to meet their ultimate real friend. Maybe that only real friend has yet to be born.

Listen.

The last to die has yet to be born. Snoozing in my chair the other night and that statement brought me to my senses. *News at Ten* was on and they were reporting on some ubiquitous famine/drought and to demonstrate the enormity of the disaster the newscaster came out with that line. Reporting from the scene of the crime he made of it a theatre, and inviting viewers to put pen to cheque book, my response was to reach for pen and paper and scribble down his quote with a view to future plagiarism. Then I went back to sleep.

You won't tell my friends, will you?

Half the world is starving to death and most of us don't care. Not really. We sit through the nightly ritual on the news and tut-tut and shake our heads but have largely dismissed the nightmare visions by the time the kettle's boiling for the Horlicks. We are a selfish hemisphere Meg, in that we tolerate mass starvation but not the train running five minutes late.

I was trying to tell my wife this last night but she told me to wheesh because she couldn't hear the weather forecast. She went to bed after that and I sat up all hours watching telly. As a consequence I smoked too much and now I'm half way through my last cigarette. I think I'm half way to becoming nocturnal, but whatever, a trot to the shop is in order. Wednesday is *Standard* day so there is always the job page to be perusing. Dad had two jobs, I have none. Maybe I'm being made to pay the price for earlier paternal greed?

Joke! The money he earned left him little choice. You know, he had a sister who he denied too, until about a month before he died. He had cancer but he was never told but he knew. He knew alright Meg. He waved me over to his bed one night and asked me to get in touch with Nellie. I hadn't a clue who Nellie was, and didn't think there was any particular relevance in what he was saying. He was all muddled up with drugs, our tragically thin dad stranded in a cloud of pillows.

But I told my mother second maybe third time he asked, and Nellie was duly summoned and arrived the next night. Everyone was greeting their eyes out. Christ, Nellie his sister, and I never even knew she existed. There had been some kind of family bust-up way back – God knows what about. But Nellie came, which is more than can be said for any of the Tory club crew. Nellie came and for years I've harboured a notion to write about that night but I daren't in case I get it all wrong and end up making people laugh.

Talking of laughs, don't you agree it was quite a howler taking receipt of my first ever UB40 on my fortieth birthday? A sort of rejection slip in pidgin English. Being unemployed is doing my head in Meg, in as much as it's making me a domesticated nutcase. I dropped some ash just then and brushing it away I was left with a great smear of dust, as well as ash, across my fingers. It was as if I had witnessed an obscenity. *When was this place last dusted?* I demanded of the cat.

Oh well, that's two tasks now await me. The acquisition of fags and newspaper, and then a return home to dust. A busy day, as they say. And if I'm feeling really benevolent I might just clean my wife's boots. They've been sitting on the back doorstep for a week now – in quarantine – covered in dog shit. Whenever I open the door and see the flash of white I think for a split second that it's the cat. Yesterday I bent down to pat them, issued a reassuring word or two before the stench brought me to my senses.

● ● ●

Home with the fags now Meg. Eventful journey to the shop
– well, eventful journey *back* to be more precise. I punctuated
the first half of the trip by waving at strangers in passing cars.
It's amazing because they almost always wave back. Try it
yourself some time. On the way home I had my nose stuck in
the *Standard* and ended up bumping into a plasterer. I knew he
was a plasterer because he was a strange colour and besides, it
said so on his van.

Amazing coincidence to bump into a plasterer because
we've been after one for ages and had been getting nowhere.
This rare plasterer was doing some work on Mrs Anderson's
bungalow, or at least what used to be her bungalow. She
moved out recently, thank God, but more on Mrs Anderson
later. Anyway, we need some plastering work done on the back
of the garage so the man with the chalk-white face is coming to
give it the once-over this afternoon.

!! Yippee – a visitor !!

We've been doing loads of work around the house. We
built a small extension to the dining room, and put a new roof
on the garage and bricked up the back of it, because the kids
were forever putting their ball through the window. This endless procession of tradesmen haven't half chomped their way
through the redundancy money though.

The good lady wife applies a weird logic to the money
situation and says the quicker it's spent the sooner we'll have
our finances in order. She says with the redundancy money to
continually fall back on I show no discipline, so once it's gone
I'll have no option but to be sensible with money. I'm inclined
to argue with her about this but only inclined to in a kind of
abstract sense, that is to say argue in her absence. When she
becomes a physical presence the notion tends to wither on me.
There is a kind of distorted wisdom in what she says, but all
the same, I'm tempted to hurl her theory the way of Brent
Hodgson. There is surely a surrealist masterpiece waiting to be
spun from such an argument.

It's academic now anyway because we're about skint. You
won't tell my friends, will you?

But I was going to tell you about Mrs Anderson. She was a
favourite primary school teacher of mine and over the years
I'd thought of her often. And then I discovered she lived just a
couple of streets away. Isn't it amazing the way life can lob
surprises at you? Anyway, I made contact with her and she

remembered me – *genuinely remembered me!* I used to pop by
for a blether and together we'd recall the rumoured good old
days and sometimes I'd even do a spot of gardening for her
because she was a frail old thing. I had found myself an old
new friend or a new old friend, depending on how you look
upon it.

But then once the novelty began to wear off I realised she
was a bit of a reactionary old stick. Horrors of horrors: old Mrs
Anderson who I idolised as a kid (she was OLD Mrs Anderson
even back then) was someone I was not particularly *fond* of.
But by then I had metamorphosed into some kind of emotional
crutch to this lonely old woman (who given the chance would
have had everyone flogged if not hung, drawn and quartered
and the black folk sent home and as for poofters and adulter-
ers…) not to mention doubling up as her fucking gardener-
cum-handyman.

In the end it was disaster. Supping tea with her one afternoon and recalling my 'Jesus Loves Me' solos at school
assemblies, I was consumed by one of my panic attacks and just
had to flee. It's true what they say about fight or flight Meg. I
couldn't very well fight so it was flight time. I told her I was
going to the toilet and just scarpered – ran home as if my life
depended upon it! And we *never ever* had any more contact. I
was too embarrassed and at a complete loss as to what to say
and God alone knows what she thought of the situation. It's
funny that she never ever phoned. (Side-splitting in fact –
would register quite a reading on the Gregor Cooper scale of
human hilarities.) After that I had to devise the strangest of
routes home to avoid walking past her house.

But as I said, the house has been sold and Mrs Anderson's
in an old folks' home now. Apparently she's round the twist,
and probably because of me. Maybe she reported me missing
to the police, ranted on at such length about a man who sang
'Jesus Loves Me' going missing in her toilet that they decided
she was crazy and had her certified. I found out she was in an
old folks' home by employing subterfuge with the new occu-
pants. I spun them a silly yarn which was such a silly yarn that
for a while I still had to take strange routes home to avoid passing the house. After a bit I gave up caring, but if I need advice
in the future on tracking people down I'll contact you Meg.

Incidentally, by some strange coincidence Mrs Anderson is
in the same old folks' home as Aunt Nellie, who I've had virtu-

ally no contact with since dad died. I've occasionally thought
about visiting her but it's out of the question now. Nellie's
mental state is unknown to me, as is Nellie herself of course.
Sad places some of those old folks' homes. Strange how they
get to call themselves 'home' when they have to take you away
from your home to put you there in the first place.

I used to know a guy who was a nurse in an old folks'
home and one old man there was forever shitting himself. My
friend Simon said there was no medical reason as to why this
should be the case, so he bribed the old man. The old man
liked a smoke so Simon told him that if he managed to stay
clean for a week he'd treat him to twenty fags. It worked a
treat. But before Simon knew what was happening all the other
old guys had started shitting themselves too.

None of *them* gave a damn whether their friends got to
know or not.

I should at this stage apologise for the amount of shit flying
around these pages. Honestly, it's not designed to put you off.
Rather, a getting to know you (me). Or maybe it represents the
situation had my mother still been alive. The shit would have
been flying by the bucket load then.

In the days (decades!) of employment I used to be lumbered
with the task of dishing out the Christmas gifts to colleagues-
become-pensioners, and old Derek who used to be warehouse
manager had ended up in an old folks' home. (Christ, it seems
the choice is one of dropping dead in the off-licence or living
long enough to be dumped in the old folks' home!)

But old Derek. He has completely wandered. Last time I
saw him he was breaking his heart when I left because he'd
thought I was his son coming to take him home. He kept asking me to fetch his suitcase. The staff, some of them at least,
thought it funny. One woman in particular didn't just find it
funny but thought for some reason that I should find it funny
too. She was as fat as a pig and stank like one and I knew for
sure that once I'd gone she'd be into the big tin of biscuits I'd
left for the old boy.

The poor old sod. He was gawking out the window and
waving as I drove off. If I had taken him home I wonder if he
would ever have twigged that I wasn't really his son? Makes
you shudder, the bleak and isolated world some old folks are
forced to inhabit. Not just old folks. My neighbour who committed suicide used to complain about loneliness yet there was

over two hundred people at his funeral. (I got to sing about
Jesus at that assembly too, but it was far from being a solo.)
This planet is teeming with people and it's teeming with people
who are desperate to make contact with others. Some are more
desperate than others and some have reasons more desperate
than others.

You know Meg, I hadn't much time for most of the folk I
was forced to share my working day with and now I can't start
to describe how much I miss them. All their little mannerisms
and foibles and quirks (I know, I know, tautology – you've
told me often enough) which drove me crazy, I now hanker
after. I wonder how their wives and husbands and cats and
dogs are doing. In a way we were all made to share each other's
domestic habitat (not to mention habits, but now I do) and
while bored senseless with all the mundane detail I think we
actually became quietly addicted to our daily dose of each
other. I watch *Neighbours* every evening and every evening
announce how ghastly the whole spectacle is. But I watch it
every evening Meg.

You won't tell my friends, will you?

But the folk at work. Maybe we didn't like each other at
times but we were all each other had to share the days with.
When the place first closed we continued making arrangements
to meet. We'd gather as a big group and go to the Job Centre
together, drink a defiant beer or two and then congregate for
thirty *Special Business Lunches* in the Chinese. We must have
looked like a coach party. This went on for a good few weeks
until I think we began to feel slightly ridiculous about the situation. Then the solidarity began to fall apart and we retreated
into our individual uselessness.

You know, I can't recall the names of any of the folk who
shared the white space of our dad's daytime job. Just those
from the twilight zone. Those who in comparison with where
he came from were fairly well-off and enjoyed a degree of
local esteem. How come the old man befriended them and
talked about them so often when politically they were poles
apart? Maybe because they had so much to disagree about
and in consequence had plenty to talk about? Maybe the daytime mob agreed about everything and spent all day just
nodding at each other. Like one of those fairground attractions
which featured open-mouthed plastic clowns, whose heads
simply rotated from side to side and then went bobbing up

and down. (Nice internal rhythm to that sentence – *Ed*.)

But the folk at work again. (See? I can't let go of them.) Without realising it we formed some kind of homogenous group, and now the place has closed we've been scattered. Together we represented something, but now ... you never realise just how much self-identity is tied up in what you DO, in what you ARE. I used to be a busy man but it was never hard going. Now I've no job and nothing much to do all day and believe me Meg, that IS hard going. To think I used to hanker after more time to write. Now I've all the time in the world to write but something doesn't feel right.

It's a kind of paradox. I feel that I won't write anything of worth until I have to struggle and fight to find the time in which to write in. And there doesn't seem much immediate chance of a job, certainly not in the old trade. None of us have much chance of acquiring work back in the old trade so whatever we end up doing we'll basically be pretending. *This is what I work at but it isn't what I am.* As if I'd taken that old man home with me and we'd pretended to be father and son.

Anyone can go through the motions. Even my son hidden behind a dry-stane dyke, but Meg, my fear is that all you and I will end up doing is *going through the motions*. We might just pretend – or even worse, pretend to pretend. I think it best that we proceed slowly, but proceed we *must*. Whatever, there will be no rejection slip from me.

Our dad pretended he didn't have a sister but when he reached the door marked EXIT he wanted that lie exposed. Maybe the reason so much literature is rooted in misery is because writers want the lie exposed too. And it's up to each and every writer to define what they see as the lie. You were near fifty before you discovered what the big lie was in your case Meg, and for the life of me I can't work out what your mother thought she was achieving in revealing it to you. (We're back to kids and automatic assumptions again, in this case yours. I suppose that was the lie she had to expose.)

I think the lie for me must have something to do with waving at strangers in passing cars. And the truth is perhaps rooted in the need to flee in breathless panic from the home of an old woman and thereafter trailing home via back streets. Exploring a new geography.

By writing I both explore and reinvent my history. My history includes a vision of our dying father stranded in bed and he in turn was stranded with the memory of a sister. He was trapped too with the history of his having rejected her, and I wonder now who else was in there jostling for his attention.

My history has amongst its constituent parts my fleeing a frail old woman who as well as having taught me to read and write, provided me with my early history and geography lessons. And it includes finding a friend slumped across the steering wheel of his car as it fed him death through a hosepipe. This was how he chose to relax at home, such was his despair.

That history reverberates with the drunken laughter of assorted Tories as our dad hob-nobbed with the class enemy. In there too is the cruelty of so-called caring professionals, sneering as an old man begged me for an identity when all I could offer him was a tin of biscuits to suck on. That history had me trail the streets as part of a redundant and bewildered coach party, and finally it delivered me to where I'm at right now. All caught up in remembering and turning my attention to you. Addressing what you *are*. This is the present but I am more concerned with the past which colours this present. I cannot fathom out whether a history dies with a death or is born of it. My history is my geography and together they are my language.

But you wouldn't let me tell my friends, would you Meg? At least, not very often. I must have been using a language that was foreign to you then, a language you are so suddenly keen to learn. Back then you used to send me your regrets – on a little rejection slip. And that little rejection slip would have this printed along the bottom: SORRY, BUT KEEP ON TRYING.

And I guess that's what this whole business must be for you Meg – *trying*. Normally an editor can simply blue pencil anything they don't like but not on this occasion. On this occasion you're stuck with it. Not just a word or a line or even a paragraph, but the whole fucking shooting match. Chapter and verse.

You're stuck with me, stuck with him. Our father, eh? I wonder if he *is* in heaven? Maybe he doesn't deserve to be, or then again, it's maybe the case that an extra-marital leg-over isn't such a sin in the grand scheme of things. I certainly hope Jesus still loves *him*. And after all, they were desperate times – World Wars have a lot to answer for. What did you do during the war dad? Mm... quite.

Beats killing people I suppose. If your mum and our dad were still alive we could have had enormous fun reintroducing them. Could have had them bunged up together in some old folks' home. I wonder what he would have said to her? JESUS CHRIST WOMAN I NO RECOGNISE YOU AT FIRST WITH YOUR CLOTHES ON. And I didn't recognise **you** at first either, but we're in this together whether we like it or not. I'm exploring a history I *thought* I both knew and understood, whereas you are delving into a history that was – for me at least – already history.

But take care Meg, and be patient. Through time we'll get to know where we really stand in relation to each other. (Hybrid siblings is a term comes to mind.) Incidentally, there's two things I'm desperately curious to know, now that the truth has finally caught up with us. The first is this: what effect has all this had on the memory of the man you *thought* was your father? And, secondly, I don't really care whether you tell my friends or not.

But will you tell yours?

Moira Forsyth

GOOD WIVES

My mother had been dying for months. She would not do it in Edinburgh, where my sister Anne lived, or in Inverness, where I was, but insisted on staying in Aberdeen, through a long harsh winter. During the week my Aunt Elizabeth shopped for her and the district nurse came in every day. On alternate weekends, Anne and I travelled to Aberdeen to clean the house, change the bed and iron our way through seven night-dresses, three bedjackets and last week's sheets and towels. By February, we were exhausted, and had begun to wish she would either die, or become so ill she'd no longer be able to argue if we insisted on her going into hospital at last. And yet, we were terrified of both these things.

We did not even have the comfort of each other's company, Anne and I. We had two phone calls a week. The Sunday night call went like this:

'I'm home.'

'How was she?'

'The same.'

'The same?'

'The poinsettia's dead. Didn't you water it?'

'I can't remember. Did she notice?'

'Oh yes.'

'Anything else?'

'She needs some more scarlet.'

'Is that what it's called – just scarlet?'

'Oh God, I think so. It's bright red, anyhow. And she's nearly out of the yellow as well. The pale one, but I don't know what that's called.'

'I'd better ring her, Anne, and ask.'

'Right. Speak to you on Thursday. Better go – kids are starving.'

The Thursday conversation, before Anne or I drove to Aberdeen next day, you can imagine for yourself. We said more about our own lives then, for we'd lived them all week. On Sunday night, one of us had been living our mother's life, and the other was so relieved not to be doing it herself, she could think about nothing else.

Our husbands learned to cook roast beef and chicken, and

our children to pare potatoes and use the washing machine, so
that their sports kit was clean for school after Saturday's rugby
or swimming. I suppose it was good for them. At first we made
pies and casseroles, had our own ironing up to date and left
lengthy messages on the kitchen table. But as the weeks
stretched into months, this efficiency broke down. We all got
used to instant meals and crumpled clothes. When the cancer
had been diagnosed in October we thought she would be dead
by Christmas. The doctors had been grave, unhopeful, her
collapse into helplessness sudden and frightening. So we fully
expected that our mother would ruin this Christmas, and many
to come, by dying either just before, or actually on Christmas
Day itself. But we had always underestimated her tenacity. Her
grip on life was fierce and determined. And thus we learned
that her hold on us was still unyielding too.

In February, the snow was so bad Graham wanted me to
take the train, or not to go at all.

'Get the nurse in,' he said. 'Dammit to hell, we could *pay*
for a nurse.'

He was getting tired of being left every other weekend; so
was Ian, down in Edinburgh.

'I'd better go,' was all I said. 'She needs the embroidery
threads, anyway.'

'Why can't Elizabeth get them?'

'She's colour blind – Mum doesn't trust her.' I sighed. 'You
know that.'

'Tell her to read a book instead,' he said, going out.
'Bloody embroidery.'

But my mother had never liked reading. I can remember
her standing between our twin beds when we were children,
saying,

'I don't know what you find in these books you're always
reading. It's late. Put your lights out.'

When she had gone downstairs, we'd put the bedside lamp
on and start again. We liked the same books; our favourite was
Little Women. I was always Jo; Anne was sometimes Meg,
sometimes (when she'd had one of her chest infections) Beth.
Really, she wanted to be Jo as well, but I had claimed her and I
was older. We took it in turns to read bits of the story out to
each other. We were in love with Laurie, and longed for a
brother as the March girls did; we got angry with Amy (neither
of us wanted to be her) and never forgave her for destroying

Jo's stories; most of all, we adored their mother, the perfect, wise and loving Marmee. Eventually, our copy of *Little Women* came to pieces, and one day, after a long spell of not even thinking about it (we were fourteen, reading Regency romances now) I discovered our mother had thrown it out. She was quite unrepentant. 'Goodness,' she said, 'it was in tatters. And filthy. I had a good clear out while you were on yon school trip. I must have got rid of it then, with the other rubbish.'

We bought another copy, of course, but it was never the same, too shiny and hard, the pages no longer falling open flat and reassuring at our favourite passages.

Reading, when I think of it, would have been too *still* an occupation for my mother. She had more energy than any woman I've ever known. Most of it was expended on house-work. When she did sit down in the evening her hands went on being busy. She took up embroidery as soon as we were old enough for her to leave it lying around, the needle poked out at the last stitch, sharp and vertical amongst delicate flowers and ferns.

At the beginning of March there was a thaw, and I drove down slowly through a landscape still white, but pock-marked with rain, the trees dripping, slush piled like wet brown sugar by the side of the road.

I put my key in the door and went in, legs trembling slightly from the long drive, and set my bag down in the hall. There was, as always, a smell of stale food and furniture polish. I opened the kitchen window and one in the living room, and went upstairs.

'Is that you?' she called.

'Yes, I'm here. How are you?'

Her pillows had slipped since the district nurse's call that afternoon. She tried to raise herself and tilted her white cheek, soft and cool, for my kiss.

'How were the roads?'

'All right.'

'There's soup,' she told me. 'Elizabeth brought me soup for my lunch, and she said there's some left.'

'Yes, I can smell it.' She sniffed sharply.

'Did you open the windows?'

'Yes.'

'Don't let the place get chilled then.'

I adjusted her pillows and brought fresh water and her tablets. She gulped; it was hard now for her to swallow. Then she lay back, and her skin was only just creamier than the pillow, only just flesh and not paper.

'I'll get on then,' I said. 'Do you want anything?'

'Just my hot milk.'

'I'll bring it up at nine.'

Silently, she watched me go.

Downstairs, Elizabeth had left a huddle of dishes in the sink. They were scummy and cold, difficult to wash. The house was chilly now, so I closed the windows and turned up the heating before I set to work to clear the kitchen. Elizabeth was my father's sister. She was not like my mother: she had no housewifely skills and was quite unconcerned about leaving a mess for other people to clear up. In this, and in other ways, she reminded me of my children. But she was cheerful, and I was glad when she came in on Saturday to see me, even if I had to hoover round her in the hall while she dripped water on the carpet from her umbrella and talked about her cats.

'I dinna ken why you bother,' she said, as I switched off and rewound the flex. 'She's only as far as the bathroom now. She wouldn't know there was dust lying.'

'She'd know,' I said. Elizabeth shrugged.

'Ach well, it's your funeral.' She saw no humour in this and remained unembarrassed, unpacking biscuits from her bag.

'I'll mak' us a fly cup,' she offered. 'These ginger creams are awful fine. Would Susan like one, d'you think?'

'You could try,' I said, but knew Elizabeth would have to take the rest of the packet home with her. My mother ate almost nothing now.

'I'm staying on till Monday this time,' I told my aunt as we sat in the kitchen drinking tea. 'The doctor's coming in.'

'She's a marvel, your mother.' Elizabeth leaned forward. There were biscuit crumbs on the corners of her mouth, caught in the fine white hairs on her upper lip. Her skin, like my mother's, had the downy softness of old age, the lines fine, as if her face had been crumpled up, then smoothed out again.

'Yes,' I said. 'She'll see the spring at this rate.'

'Oh well.' Elizabeth shook her head and helped herself to another ginger cream. 'I've my doubts about that.' Hope sprang up; I could not help it. 'You think –'

'Och, you can see for yourself,' she told me through a

crumbling mouthful. 'She's a poor thing now.'

When I went upstairs my mother had touched neither biscuit nor tea. She lay back on her pillows, the embroidery frame by her limp right hand, the pattern unchanged since yesterday. I felt a stab of something I might – had she been anyone else – have called pity. Or perhaps it was fear. I don't know. She was lying very still, but her dark eyes watched me as I moved about the room.

Everything was just as it had been when we were children, and when my father was alive, except that his suits no longer hung in the gentleman's wardrobe. On top lay the glass dish he put his loose change in every night, empty now except for two buttons and a pin. The mahogany of the dressing table and wardrobes still gleamed warm and polished; the carpet, though it had been replaced more than once, was still the familiar blue and green pattern, a design my mother told me was no longer being made.

'Still,' she had commented, 'this one will see me out.'

From the beginning she had referred calmly to her own death, just as matter of fact as she had always been when other people died – even my father.

'He's comfortable now,' she said, her gaze direct and tearless, challenging Anne and me with our blotched faces, who had sniffled all through the funeral, and sobbed openly at the graveside.

Now I lit her lamps and drew the curtains, making the room dim and shadowy. The solid shapes of the furniture loomed, but like old friends, keeping her company.

'I've not long,' she said suddenly as I was leaving the room.

'What?'

'I need nursing now,' she said, 'but it'll not be for long.'

What was she saying? I came back and sat not on the bed (a thing she disliked) but on the edge of the blue Lloyd loom chair with its faded cushion.

'Elizabeth can't cope – it'll have to be you and Anne.'

'But –' I began, then stopped. I guessed what she wanted: to have either Anne or me here all the time. 'There's the hospital,' I said, not wanting to utter the word 'hospice', though she knew that was what I meant.

'No,' she said. 'I'll not go to strangers, not now.'

'But Mum –' I hesitated. 'There's the children – and my job – and – look we could get you a nurse. Graham suggested a private nurse. What about that?'

If she had had the strength to snort, that's what she'd have done. But she made do with a curl of her lip.

'Nurse!' she scoffed. Then her face twisted with pain; she leaned forward, retching, waving her hand helplessly, unable to speak. But I knew – I ran for the bowl, got there just in time. Her body heaved, back arched, ribs expanding, belly concave, but there was nothing for her to vomit up but saliva, and a trace of bile. I wiped her face with a damp cloth, helped her lie back.

'Oh,' she gasped, 'oh.' Round her mouth, the skin was bluish, even in the lamplight.

'I'll speak to the doctor,' I said, 'and Anne. But I don't know how we'll manage.'

'You'll manage,' she answered, her voice faint but still firm.

We did, of course. Anne had no job at the time, and I did, so she was there during the week and I went down at weekends. Elizabeth covered the gaps between one of us leaving and the other arriving.

'That's fine,' was all my mother said, when Anne explained the arrangements to her. But when Anne tried to embrace her, to show there was love in our efforts, not just duty, she drew back, wincing. She hurt, she said. Everything hurt.

But still she did not die. Our marriages creaked under the strain; our boys grew remote as only adolescents can, retreating to their bedrooms amid a festering pile of unwashed clothes and computer games. Our daughters were by turns sulky and rude, and pathetically dependant. Most of their complaints began with the words *Everyone else's mother...*

Anne and I spoke on the telephone more often, but more briefly. There were no demands now for embroidery thread, only the complex routine of medication to communicate and explain.

'She's so thin,' we would say to each other. 'There's nothing of her. I don't know how she can go on.' She frightened us now, her skin damp with sweat, her eyes black ringed with pain. But she herself did not yield. We were the ones who wept, driving home, hardly able to see the road, too tired to think.

Then, in April, on a day so warm I was driving with my window three inches down, between Anne's going and my coming, and while Elizabeth took thrifty cuttings from my mother's geraniums, she died at last.

Anne came back up next day, on the train. Ian said he would drive north on Tuesday for the funeral, and then take her home. We had the weekend to sort things out.

'We'll get it over,' I said. 'No sense coming back again. The house can go on the market next week, and we'll sort out the furniture once it's sold.'

'I feel so light,' Anne said, 'as if I'd been on some sort of starvation diet. Lightweight, light-headed.'

'It's shock,' I said. 'I feel the same.'

'No.' She came and hugged me and I inhaled her spicy scent, her clean hair, speckled with grey, brushing my face. 'No – it's relief.'

I hugged her back; we almost laughed.

We could not have said these things if our mother had still been in the house. But when Mr Macintyre came up from the funeral directors we told him we did not want her to stay here. Lying in rest, was what he called it. She would lie in rest somewhere else.

We cleared our old room too, of all the books and toys left for our children to play with on visits to Granny. They'd outgrown them all now and most we consigned to the Oxfam pile.

Anne found the copy of *Little Women* – the new, hardly-read one.

'Do you want this?' she asked. 'Someone gave it to Jane for her birthday last year. Not that she's bothered with it – she's not much of a reader.'

'All right,' I said. 'Lucy might like it.' I was thinking, though, that I'd read it myself.

'Remember,' I asked Anne, 'the picture on the front of the old copy? On the dust jacket.'

'Yes,' she said. 'Jo had a red dress and Meg's was blue.'

'And Amy's blonde ringlets –'

'And Beth with a cat on her lap.'

'And Marmee.'

'She had such a nice face, Marmee.' Anne sat down on what had once been her own bed. 'Terribly kind and patient.'

'Loving,' I said.

'Remember how cross Mum was when we cried about Beth being ill?'

'She thought we were crazy – crying about something that happened in a book.'

'Well,' Anne sighed, 'she didn't like people to cry about

things that happened in real life either.'

'*They* seemed real, didn't they – Marmee and all those girls?'

'Yes,' Anne said, 'they did.'

We sat there, Anne on her bed, me on mine, fingering the worn candlewick, gazing at the piles of books and toys on the floor and thinking about Marmee and the March girls.

'Come on.' I stood up, rousing us both. 'We'd better get this done.'

After the funeral – a cold day again, with a sharp easterly wind – Anne and I drove home with our husbands.

A few days later Lucy came across *Little Women*, lying on top of the box of books I'd taken from my mother's house.

'Laura's read this,' she said. 'She says it's great. Can I have it?'

'I brought it for you.'

Later, I found her lying on her stomach on the floor, already at page fifty.

'Do you like it?' I asked.

'What?' She had the dazed look of someone dragged back from another world.

'Oh yeah. It's good. Except for the mother.'

'How do you mean?'

'Marmee. Sounds like a cat's name. And she's so goody goody. Not like any mother *I* ever came across.'

'She's a sort of ideal mother,' I said vaguely. 'Loving, kind...'

'Aw hey – she never nags or yells at her kids, she never shows them up in front of their friends – she's not *real*.'

'Well...' I began feebly. 'Well, some mothers probably are like that.'

Lucy shook her head firmly.

'No,' she said. 'Take it from me. I'm an expert on mothers.'

'Oh,' I said. 'Right.'

After supper, Anne phoned.

'How are you?' she asked.

'Fine,' I said. 'How are you?'

'Fine.'

There was a pause.

'That's a lie,' she said.

'Yes. Me too.'

'I feel guilty,' Anne sighed. 'That's how I feel.'

'Yes, that's the word.'

Another pause.

'She was hard on us,' Anne offered.

Well, we never had much... response,' I went on, backing her up. 'Not much... loving.'

'It's just –'

'I know.'

'Well, then, say it. Save me saying it.'

But we said it together. *We should have done more.* The words hung there, suspended somewhere between Edinburgh and Inverness. Probably around Aberdeen. We should have done more.

Only, this was not the truth either. What we meant, but could not say, was that we should have *felt* more. But that was something not even guilt could alter now.

Raymond Friel

from GREENOCK FROM OLD PHOTOGRAPHS

Inverkip Street Graveyard

The 'pavèd beds'
Were being turned over
At such a rate
And the fresh dead
Being frogmarched
Back through the gate –
Bewildered, sore,
A 'snatcher' on either side –
That the appalled citizens
Banded together a flying squad
And named it,
In the grand evasive style
Of Guild Hall,
The Greenock Free Gardeners' Society.
The graveyard was ringed
With burning braziers –
The 'gardeners', greasy with fear,
Huddled under the cloak
Of a dripping yew tree.
Stowed in the darkness
Of a dubious rig,
Tight-shrouded, fleeced cadavers
Journeyed upriver
To a new life.

The Albert Harbour

The works' tracks
Disappeared into sludge.
As had a few workers.
The 'soil' dredged
From the viscous riverbed
Was carted to Campbell Street
To make a promenade
For watercolourists
And parasol-twirling daughters
Of sugar barons.
The footnotes mention
That during construction
East Clyde Street was 'cleared';
That five hundred gentlemen
Sat down to dinner
And a programme
Of over twenty toasts and replies;
That the harbour was home
To river steamers
For the winter months.

River steamers and their perfect reflections.

The Visit of the Channel Fleet

The lights of HMS Minotaur
Winked in the dead calm of the estuary.
In the flushed drawing room
Of Whitefarland
English officers curled their hands
Round glasses of malt.
Kinipple's daughters
Sat around the piano forte –
Tutored, biddable,
Lost in a flaring, labyrinthine darkness.

William Gilfedder

OBLOMOVISM

This was supposed to be a long critical poem
About a lazy so and so good for nothing
Who spends his entire life day-dreaming
Until one day he falls in love
And has to face up to the harsh realities of life.
But after 12 hours of lying in a hammock
Feet curled up in a pair of Turkish slippers
And a genuine Persian saddle bag for a pillow
I just don't have the energy to write any more
So please (if it's not too much trouble)
Will somebody hold a match to the burner under the kettle
I'm coming down for a cup of tea.

John Glenday

ANNUNCIATION

And this was their appearance; they had the likeness of a man.
And every one had four faces, and every one had four wings.

We were discussing the construction of an angel's wings.
She'd found that old print of The Annunciation
where they arch above his head like an angry swan's
and cast down radiants of gold-coloured light on the hapless
                                                            virgin.

She said feathers must mean angels were reptilian, essentially,
but if angels were fashioned on the lines of a god,
as we were, then surely they should be mammalian, and their
                                            wings, (if indeed
these are to be taken as more than mere bright conventions of
                                                            artistry

like haloes, or the holy spirit hovering with a hawk's jizz)
their wings should be skin fixed on a framework of canted
                                                            bone,
something like fruit bats or devils. *Quod erat demonstrandum,*
she said. *You know: qui mane oriebaris?*

She said that if angels had wings and if angels really were,
then in her opinion their wings would be like the wings of
                                                            moths
which at rest lie open to display the stains of their stippled
                                                            faith
like bark, or lichen, or wheatfields viewed from the air.

Angels hanker after light like moths, she said, but they hate
                                                            the sun
and painlessly shed their talc. She said she imagined
if ever we touched them with our hands,
no matter how hard they tried, they would never quite fly
                                                            again.

BLIND

I was thinking of what you said
and it isn't true. Who can say what will come
and what will come to nothing?

I realise how far away you were –
that shell moon long set, but its voice calling
through the half-open window

and the form that lay beside me in the bed
no more than an absence smoothed into the dark.
That night, I held you not for warmth or pardon, but for light.

Remember the blind man
who passed us in our street?
How he paused once to touch his stick gently

against the world – just to confirm it still
travelled with him – then strode on as if something
that was not darkness lay ahead?

NIMBUS
i.m. Davy Brown

In Tibetan Buddhism, the symbol for the mind's creative power
is not a light bulb, as in the Beano, but a cloud.
And I've heard that in Mexico they believe the dead
may speak from their graves for a short while after rain.
But Skye is nothing like Mexico.
They would never fall silent here.
Then perhaps it's true.

When I was seven, my father explained
how the dead converse through the telegraph wires
and it's only because we're stuck with being alive
that we can't understand what they say.
When I hugged the pole with him and listened,
their speech was thin and distant, but as heavenly as song.

A friend once described how he stood above Bernisdale
in a winter storm and watched the waves beat themselves
white against the gale, then surge up into the sky and disappear.
He said a blackface ewe went floundering past his door like
                                             tumbleweed.

I believe whatever has been done can only be translated, never
                                             undone.
That day, rain tasted salt at Invermoriston.

Rody Gorman

MU CHARADAL

Shìos mu Charadal air sgrìob dhuinn
'S ann a dhealaich sinn fad tacain
Ri linn gnè de ghradan-uisge

'S thog mi orm leam fhìn
Air feadh an fhraoich loisgte
'S nan cuiseagan seargte

San talamh àrd air cùlaibh
Chùil na h-Airigh
Fo fhàileadh fann de roid

Agus a-staigh mun tìr bho acarsaid
A bha 'm fasgadh an ròid
Fo Rubh' an Iasgaich

Dh'fheuch mi ri bruthaich nach bu chas
'S am fraoch a' suathadh bacaidh ri mo chois
'S fiadh gun langanaich air stùc fad' às

'S mhothaich mi gràn-aigein
'S e a' fàs gu teann air bàrr na talmhainn
'S a' deàrrsadh na ghrian

Agus biadh-eòinein
Gun choltas dochainn ann
Na chromadh fon a' ghrèin

Agus aon t-sobhrag leatha fhèin
Fo sgàil nam freumhan
Nach maireadh ach tiotan

'S cha do chuir mi ceist carson
Ach chrom mi gus a buain
'S a toirt air ais dhut fhèin.

Maggie Graham

Novel Extract from WIRED TO THE MOON

This is the time of year when the district resounds to the sound of popping hymens. There's no danger of me adding to the cacophony, mine popped a long time ago. Anyway, mature students don't have time for bedsit passion.

I'm in the downstairs coffee bar. Wee Betty's back behind the counter, shouting Cupuramug son? Cupuramug hen? confusing the foreign students. The place is packed with new students; freshers, they're called, like wee sweeties. Wandering around in their stiff denim jackets and shiny Docs, lugging huge great bags for all those big important books. Give them a month and they'll all be Goths with Peckam's carrier bags. This will be the last time I witness a mass influx of freshers. My final year; two terms and then the finals. God, the finals. A week of hysteria, and four years over, finished. Then what?

I watched Elaine come in. She's laden with books and bags and God knows what else; she'll have aerobics or something later on. She looks lost, then she sees me and pushes through, balancing a mug and duntin big boys on the head with her Next duffel bag.

Hi. How ye doin? God Lizzie, I dinnae believe we're back here.

Elaine's East coast, I'm West, and in this bloody place the two met. She looks round at all the lost children,

Wee souls, she says.

She used to be a midwife.

I say, I hate them. Hate them because I envy them; all clean and new with everything in front of them. I can't lose my virginity in a flat in Bank Street, to some wee wanker who spouts Sartre and Proust and then comes in ten seconds; and not know that he's a wee wanker, and not know that the sex is lousy, and not know that he talks a load of pretentious shite. I would love to be that ignorant.

She smiles, then asks the inevitable.

How are things?

And I press my lips together and drag the answer up from somewhere in the region of my breastbone, where it lives.

Terrible. Now that he's at home all the time, he can object. When he was only there at weekends he didn't see. Now, with this new job, he rolls in drunk and criticises, accuses me of trying to castrate him. He sees me studying, he sees that the house is a tip, and now he'll see that it's Jill who's there when the kids get back from school. This year is going to be murder.

She reaches across and pats my hand.

How are the kids?

They're fine. Lisa's settled in well at secondary school. The other two are just the same; Carrie's fighting fit, and David's driving us all daft, but they're fine. They don't suffer.

The hand squeezes mine.

I know. Of course they dinnae. Now you sit there, and I'll get you another coffee.

Her moon and star earrings tinkle when she puts the mugs down, and I admire them.

They were a present, she says, good luck for my final year.

Who from?

She looks down into her cup and says,

Martin.

Martin is the man who broke her heart when he left her after three years. He now lives with a twenty-two year old legal secretary.

I say, What the hell is he buying you presents for?

Oh, she says, he says that I'm still part of his life. If I just hang in there, things'll be fine.

Hang in for what, Elaine? Till he stops shagging somebody else?

Her eyes fill, tears brimming over, and I feel bad. I envy her too; mine are all dammed up somewhere. I need to get out of here.

C'mon, I say. We need to move: grant queue, bank, book shop, library. Where are you going?

She says, I've got a tutorial at three. I need to go to the library. What train will you be getting back to Saltcoats?

Quarter past four.

We arrange to meet up later; and we pick up our bags and ourselves, and we leave. We stop at the library steps and she says,

Oh fuck, Lizzie. I'm scared. Are you?

Who me? Naw. Never.

And we giggle like two wee lassies. Then she goes off clutching Durkeim's theories on suicide, and I walk down the hill, against an oncoming tide of freshers.

The grant queue stretches for bloody miles, I'm here for the day. Two big hands grip my shoulders; Tony. I check for the volume of poetry... yes... Rimbaud.

So, auld yin, he says, they actually let you back in.

We both like to make a big deal of the seven years between us. Exchanging insults is our way of covering up the secret we share: we shouldn't really be here; we're impostors.

Shut it, son.

He grins down at me. Then, he has to say it.

Well hen, this is it. Come April: nine exams in eight days. Think you're up to it?

I shoot him a world weary look.

No bother, honey. No bother.

We inch forward. A to M left – M to Z right.

He lights up a Camel, puts the packet back in the pocket of his long black coat, and asks,

Who's your tutor?

James Brown.

Oh, very fucking funny.

It is. Tony, stop looking at me like that, you're making me laugh. It is, it's James Brown. This new guy: Doctor James Brown.

Yo Lizzie, he says, pelvic thrusting in the cloisters, Sex Machine.

I wish, I say, he looks like Ted Moult.

Who the fuck's he?

Oh forget it.

• • •

The winos are back in the lane. They probably never left; I'm the one who hibernates in summer. I've heard them,

See up at the Uni? See that wee lane? Students. Overflowin wi social fuckin conscience. An the wans that drink in the fancy wine bars? A couple of bob's fuck all tae they cunts.

One of them starts jigging when he sees me,

There she is... Doris Day.

I say, Away to hell; she's a virgin.

And he laughs, cackling till he nearly coughs his lungs up. Then he's away again, jigging.

I'll gie ye a wee song, hen.

'Close your eyes and I'll kiss you, tomorrow I'll miss you, remember I'll always be true.'

Christ, he's not as old as he looks. Child of the sixties:
Doris at the flicks, and The Beatles top of the pops.
Any spare change, doll?
No, I say, I've got weans to keep.
His manner changes, as he exaggerates amazement.
Oh pet, I'm so sorry. I never wid huv asked ye. Ye don't
look auld enough, that's whit it wis. I thought ye wur wan a
they fuckin students.
Laughing, so did I, I give him the fifty pence I had ready in
my hand, and as I walk towards the Underground, I can hear
him Godblessin me and my weans all the way down the lane.
Then.
'All my lovin, I will send to yooooo, all my lovin, darlin
I'll be true.'
Hey, big man. Yer the spit a Jimmy Dean, so ye are. Any
spare change?

● ● ●

The four fifteen from Glasgow Central gets me home by five
thirty. In the back door, the kitchen's tidy. My domestic help is
a little treasure. She likes kids, she likes money; we're sorted.
She makes coffee and we compare notes: Yes, they've been
good, then she goes home.
Mum, I've got the Girl's Brigade and I hate it, and she's in
a huff, and he's out playing and I don't know where he is.
She lies stretched out on her front on the carpet. Young
enough still to believe that I can fix everything.
Right Lisa, I say, Why do you hate the Girl's Brigade?
It was his mother's idea anyway. Anything to ally them
with the Church of Scotland, against their papish mother.
She says, Because that woman shouts at me.
Well don't go then. You don't need to be shouted at.
She has never needed to be shouted at. Still not pacified,
she pleads,
Will you phone up and will you tell my Nana?
Yes, I'll phone up. And to hell with your Nana. Now, why
is Carrie in a huff?
Because one of her feet's bigger than the other one.
I say, Well Lisa, I can't do anything about that; I'll talk to
her. David's in next door; I saw him when I came in. So, henny
penny, now that we've sorted all your problems, what are you
up to?

I'm going down to Mandy's. She's got the new Wet Wet Wet tape.

Wooo. Wish I was going, I say.

And she smiles. God what a smile. Hang onto it hen.

She goes away happy; and I drink cold coffee, and phone the sergeant major, and fix the huff with promises of fantastic shoes, and think and try not to think. He's working till seven. We'll see him at ten, maybe eleven. Depends.

• • •

The kids are in bed and I'm in this chair. I hate this bloody chair. I've got the paper; the one with the big pages, the one he hates... Where the hell's the Record?... Or are we too good for that now?...

My mug has COFFEE printed across it in large letters: I MUST ONLY DRINK COFFEE FROM THIS VESSEL.

I even have a book: Twentieth Century Women Poets... That pish... I have everything I could possibly need beside this chair. This chair was cleverly designed to allow me to kill myself in comfort. My mother moved from a chair to a bed to a coffin without a moment's thought. I think too much, that's my trouble. I can't get comfortable.

I tried, I really tried; but when the weans stopped sharing this chair with me, the four of us, and Topsy and Tim and Billygoat Gruff, then this chair just didn't feel right. I liked the chairs at night school, they were comfortable. Then I decided to try other chairs, see how they felt: library chairs, lecture theatre chairs, nice tutorial room chairs. I'm the Goldilocks of the University, but I'm only allowed in Daddy Bear's bed. There are more chairs that I would love to try: opera/theatre seats, train/plane seats, nice creases/sharp laps. Yes.

I hear his key. Other men bring home fish suppers or Indian carry outs; Colin Burns brings tension, bags of it. He stands there, filling the doorway. He fills every doorway.

Aye, he says, I see you're busy, as usual.

Absence and sarcasm are his only weapons. He would never hit a woman, but if he starts tonight, I could brain him with Twentieth Century Woman Poets; plead poetic justice.

Are the weans alright?

No, they died of neglect. Of course they're alright. They're always alright.

Oh aye, he says, I forgot. You're the perfect mother.
It's just not bloody fair; but then, it never has been.
I say, How the hell would you know? You're never fucking
here.
That's right. Get back to your roots. You were dragged up.
Dae all your smart pals talk like that?
Aye.
He looms over me, reeking of diesel oil and beer, spitting
words.
What is it that you want? Eh? Go on. You tell me. What is
it that you want? You don't want what other women want.
You wanted weans and now you don't want them. What is it
that you want? TELL ME.
God almighty. I don't want this. I want peace. No, I don't.
I want something, somebody. It used to be him.
I say, OK. I want more than this. I want music and poetry,
and I want laughter, and food and wine and... I want to play
the saxophone. And I want to go to... fucking... Andalucia.
AND, I want a sober man, a sober man who loves me.
He looks down at me, and I can still see the skinny
apprentice who walked me home that night. The he says,
You're no right in the heid. You are mental. You're needin
treatment. You'll get the weans taen aff you. You're wired tae
the moon, hen.
Somebody knocks at the door, and I jump up to answer it.
His mate Wullie stands there grinning at me,
Hello hen. Is the big man in?
I smile and say,
Aye. Come in.
Because I'm a nice lassie. And I grab my coat and I shout,
I'm just nipping round to Bernie's.
And I walk. I walk and I keep walking, and I don't want to
go back. I walk right down the hill, and over the railway
bridge, and round past the harbour and along the polluted
shore front. It's cold, and I can smell the sea and see the lights;
and I don't care. I don't care what I see or hear or smell or feel.
I just don't bloody care.
The big man. The fucking big man. They even call my son
wee man.
How's it goin, wee man?
Pass the ba, wee man.
Wee big man.

Nobody calls his sisters wee women. Oh that's a pretty dress, wee woman. Never. When they are women, they'll get a nice wee house, a wee family, a wee part-time job, a wee night out, a wee holiday, a wee greet, a wee cup of tea. They might need a big operation, and that'll be the highlight of their wee lives, but supposing they're ten feet fucking tall, they'll never be big women. Because, when it comes down to it, boys, size doesn't matter. Women are all wee. Next to the big man, I'm really wee and I'm shrinking by the minute. Nae bother tae the big man. I'm still walking. Walking in a circle, because I have to go back.

Back to my big lassies and my wee man.

W.N. Herbert

ROADKILL

That summer I kept hitting gulls
off the top of my windscreen
like breasting a white-hatted wave
as I sped down the country roads:
herring gulls mainly, and
their brown-speckled young,
bulky birds all, that
looking in my mirror I'd see
drop, vertically, from
an already distant impact point,
and smack upon the tarmac.

Roadkill had been bad that year:
I kept passing smears of pheasant,
well-parted rabbits' ears,
the odd pigmy mammoth, hunched by
the verge, obviously dead;
then there was the gutted angel,
small, malnourished, and
various eohippi.

On the road to Buckie one blustery day
when the sun tried bursting out
of hill-big rain-clouds, I saw
a series of creatures, half-squid, half-skate,
pale and lurid in that orangey light,
too battered to identify.

Gradually my small white car began
to alter: a membrane-like look
crept over the bumpers
as of a seabird's foot;
the hint of a pale eye glinted back
from the side mirror.
Once as I drove along
the undulant lane to Lhanbryde,
there was a rippling off the bonnet
as of feathers in a fierce breeze.

After the fifteenth gull
the seats seemed to be covered in shagreen,
a seaweed smell came off the wheel
onto my hands, and
there was an isinglass flash
to the windows.

Obviously, the car, under the impact of
so many souls, had begun to adapt.

I started slipping whitebait in
the petrol tank as a treat,
visiting the coast nightly, until
a spirit of the sandstone cliffs
by Burghead told me what to do.

That night, having strewn the back seat
with haddock and tangles, I drove
to the end of Grant Street, that looks
past the Pictish fort to the Firth,
and there asperged the dashboard
with fifteen year-old Ordiequish.
Slipping the car into first I drove,
door open, past the last houses,
lighter in my lap.

Just before the drop
I jumped, dropped the flame:
the fire quickly filled the interior
with a flicker of white wings
as the car hit the dark waters.
I watched it tumble and sink
the fifteen feet or so to liberty.

Sue Green

NEARLY A DRESS

The last time had been at her father's funeral. She remembered it quite clearly because of the occasion. In fact she would never forget because it was the only thing which had made them laugh in days. But then her family was like that, doing things differently and at the same time following form.

There were to be no flowers. She remembered being amazed when her mother, standing rigid with hands held tightly before her, told each grieving relative who called to send a donation to Oxfam instead. Watching their faces shadow with shock as they backed towards the door, she had almost felt sorry for them. But her mother was determined. There were a lot of starving people out there, some good would come of the untimeliness of it all.

A religious service wasn't even considered. Given their father's politics it was totally inappropriate. Instead his favourite classical music would be played and her brother agreed to give a short eulogy. The undertaker took it very well, commenting that the simple services were often the most meaningful. He couldn't resist suggesting though that at least one hymn be sung so that everyone could feel involved as it were. After a great deal of deliberation a consensus was reached on a composition which miraculously made no reference to God.

But there would be plenty of food, prepared and proffered to mourners in the family home. Her task was to butter one hundred and nineteen slices of bread, seventeen to a loaf, and turn them into an assortment of sandwiches. It was then she really began to wonder who funerals were for.

Her understanding was complete when her mother leaning across the table, took hold of her hand and breaking the heaviest of silences said, 'You will get something nice now, won't you. You know to wear.' It became obvious then. Funerals were for the living, not for the dead. Death is sudden, even when expected. Life just sneaks away without warning. Why should that breath be the last? Why not the next, or the one after that, or the one next week, or next year? There is a kind of indifference, a carelessness about dying, a sort of negligence that shouldn't be allowed. It's this sudden disappearance, this total abandonment which is unbearable for the living. Funerals correct all that. They bring the dead back to where they belong. Not until everyone's assembled and ready can they leave and only then on the terms of those left behind. Funerals put the living back in control.

She knew this was true as she stood in the Women's Department of the local C&A trying on the most macabre of dresses. Death had finally got her into one.

'Let's have a look then.'

She hesitated then stepped out into the lurid fluorescent lights. Her mother and sister stood staring, then suddenly broke into raucous laughter which seared through the dull murmuring of the store.

'You look like you're in drag,' were the only words she heard.

There had always been something about a dress that made her feel vulnerable. Incarcerated in one she was moulded into another persona. Her posture changed, she developed a slight swaying movement in the hips, and her arms lifted slightly. People regarded her in a different way and were horribly more polite. Often she was addressed as Mrs and a certain level of weakness presumed. Alarmingly, this someone else was always more acceptable.

She hated dresses. They were confining. They imposed limits. Give her jeans any day. And shirts and thick warm jumpers, strong boots and a heavy jacket. So what if she was constantly referred to as sonny, she knew who she was. There was the pleasure of donning leathers to journey the two hundred miles to college on her Yamaha 500. Her father would insulate her with backcopies of the Morning Star, and she would set off undeterred by ice or snow. Once, stopping to use the ladies at a roadside cafe, she caused several elderly women to leave screaming as she struggled to get her helmet off. Wearing what you wanted was fun. Dresses weren't.

Clothes say a lot. They make clear statements, describing a person instantly, without wasting any words. She had been making statements to her mother for years, but had never got a response.

'Mum, see how you think me and Janet are just good friends. Well, we're more than that. A lot more.'

Her mother leaned forward to turn the gas heater down.

'I know. I've known for a long time.'

She sat back, continuing to gaze at the lowered flame.

'Mind you, if your father was still alive I'm not sure how I would be about it.'

Her daughter stared with her into the fire.

'I don't think I've seen you in a skirt since his funeral.'

'It was a dress.'

'Hmmm. Well, there was that time you took me on holiday, and you wore that beach thing with the straps. That was a dress.'

She turned her head to meet her daughter's eyes.

'Well, nearly.'

Brent Hodgson

from PEPYS IN MY DIARY

1. Monandaeg: Today I wrote a concrete poem.

```
                    HED
            IST         AEG
        AEG                 OFT
      AND                       HEM
   MON                              ONA
```

Monandaeg is the daeg of the mona.

Glossary:
hed	head
ist	Gothic spelling of the 3rd pers. sing. of the verb to be
aeg	egg
oft	often
hem	them
mon	a Scotsman
Monandaeg	Monday
daeg	day
mona	moon
moon	a satellite useful for the measurement of time.

At this stage I wol throwe an aeppel in the watar-werks, and declare that concrete poetry is a queerios bisseness. My kenning (or cunning) of the subject I wol summarize:

1. Concrete poetry, unlic the pulp of an aeppel, is ful of indigestiblelness.
2. An aeppel is not a compound fruht.

2. Frigedaeg: Today I fund lippestick.

The lippestick was pleesant to smell:
    it mynded me of the sent of freesia.   sent: scent
I titched it with my tonge and I kent it was,
    ful of moisturising emollients.
But hwaether the lippestick wolde last an efnung,
    of eeting and drinking
    withutan federing or bledan,
    I wolde ne ken.
I have bene tolde that the lippestick,
    does nat stick to cigarettes or to glasses.
Furthermore, the lippestick hadde bene applied in twa cotes,
    to lippes that were baith clene and drie.
The lippestick that I fund,
    was on the lippes of Morag.
Sche asked me nat to telle hir husbonde of hir lippestick:
    of hir lippes of efer-lasting escarlate luke;
    of hir lippes, which sche coude pout.
Sche cyssed me agane.
    Wol you telle my husbonde? said sche.
Ne, I said;
    I wol nat telle your husbonde that you dyde spend,
    £11.50 for lippestick,
    in a handy, no frills, compact container.

3. **Today I wrote a pece of fiction mysticus.**

Today my lyf as a homo sapiens cam back to me.
I can not say why; I am content being a homo novis.
God! what a strange lyf was that, being a homo sapiens.

Morning efter morning
            endless cornflakes and cuppes of tea.
Day efter day unintelligible sounds dirling
            in my eer.
Neaht efter neaht wahting
            for the robbour cumen to my door.
Yeer efter yeer
            withutan wings to flee:
            to flee ofer the hwite shore.

4. **Today I mette a gerl – alswa a pece mystikos.**

I mette a gerl today.

Hir muid as derk as the wudd.

Her loosed clathes the cullour of deid gress.

Hir earmes were sweeping in the wind.

At hir feet lay a wraeth of snaw.

5. Today I pretended to be a Tae.

I wanted to be a Ta, but a Ta is an Anglo-Saxon Toe, and
who wolde believe me in Scotland if I said – I am a Ta! and
so I settled for the next best thyng which was a Scottish Tae.
And a Tae in Scotland is a Toe and everybuddie in Scotland
kens what a Tae is.
Weel, I howp thay do and schame on thase who do not.
There is not at the present as far as I am aware, any
ordinance forbidding the Scottish citezein from assuming the
identity of a Tae. The situation may be different in England,
as it is an independent contree with its own laws.
But as ye may ken, taking on the identity of a Tae in
Scotland is not a full-time occupation: Scotland does not
have a national theatre in which the actour can display his
or her acting skills while on the plate-forme: that is why the
Scottish public rarely gets to see a buddy portraying a Tae.
And so I walked barefoot in a Scottish field free of thistles.
And do you ken I was lucky, because there was not any
thrissels in yon field either. I walked up and doun and as I
walked, I counted my Taes:

$$1 - 2 - 3 - 5 - 6$$

and the rest of thame: I forget how many exactly. I
performed this exercise until voila! I became a Tae.
My uther Taes being redundant, mairched off this-a-wey and
that-a-wey and eventually thay made their wey up a stane
dyke to where thay had a vantage point ofer the hale field.
A stane dyke is a unique feature of the Scottish landscape,
and as I was only taute the Scottish language at the schule, I
am sorely troubled to render to the reader of English, a
precise translation of the twa words 'stane' and 'dyke'.
– And as I walked in the field, I was no longer 'me', but ane
enormous Tae.
From the top of the stane dyke I coude heer the laughter of
my uther Taes, and thay were laughing at me.
There was a bunch of my Taes on that stane dyke: I wolde
say 2 or 3 or 5 of thame at least.
And as I jigged along I heered thame count:

$$1 - 1 - 1 - 1 - 1 - 1 \dots$$

Haworth Hodgkinson

MEETING APART

Briefly together,
You and I take turns
To speak and to be silent.

Neither you nor I
Will remember what we say,
Nor even understand.

But later,
Back in our separate worlds,
Friends will notice we have
Changed slightly.

Matthew Hollis

THREE CHOICES

We all saw it. He fell out of the sky,
bouncing the lake Damnbuster style
before the friction caught up with him
and he sank like a slowing water-skier.
I told the kids to go inside
where they watched, palms to the glass.

He said he was on the run. *Oh?*
Crimes of cartography.
I imagined him chased by Ordinance Survey,
wellies, kagools and steamed up glasses.
That doesn't sound so serious? But I
was missing the rub.

I take a pen, I take a map,
and what I draw comes true, he said.
A fish turned on the surface, applauding.
There's something! And moved to prove it,
he drew a couple of contours
and raised the house two hundred feet.

He said it began when he drew out the trees
and ran a stream through the plans
the office was working on.
Next morning he found it just as he'd drawn.
And at home that night with a dark blue pen
he managed to deepen the Chilean Trench.

Other things too:
lakes and greenery for bone-dry Africa
and land to ease the pressure on Asia;
things that went on for weeks, he said,
until he began receiving visits
from people he didn't much care for.

So he ran, placing ravines behind him,
until it dawned that his only chance
was to draw them into a glen, like this,
and proceed to flood the place.
Ours, then, was a simple choice:
to leave the valley or drown.

We never talk of that. Only
sometimes, watching the kids skim stones
brings it back and then of course
the climb to the house
past the mound at the foot of the garden
where we lay flowers now and again.

RED GREEN BLUE

I saw you at the gallery
explaining the theory of colour
which rose as you spoke one to another,
dust in the hum and beam of projector.

This is the third day I've come
and you smile faintly. But by Friday
you'll grow suspicious, both of us
wondering how long this can go on.

Helen Lamb

I SWALLOWED YOUR NAME

I swallowed your name
it had to be done

first – sealed behind lips
and held on my tongue
hard-edged consonants
round pill of vowels

you didn't go down easily

small talk was impossible
with your name lodged
dangerously in my throat
I gagged on the syllables

my eyeballs bulged

it could have been fatal
but I held on till
even the thought of you dissolved
into the rhythm of my breath

you're trapped there still

a tell-tale sigh
caught between the rise and fall
but softly so
it almost passes for silence.

Katy Lironi

TERMINATION 4

THE DISCOVERY

3 July 1992

'Yes, that's positive,' announces the doctor. Efficiently. Effectively. Unleashing some effervescent emotion. Commotion. Devotion to tears and drama.
'Look. The positive sign is blue.'
Give me please a pale blue paper tissue from the pastel coloured box and let me wipe the dumbfounded tears slipping down my pregnant, trembling, silent cheeks. I am silently shaking. The tissue is wet and I am covering my soaked, hotly embarrassed face with my hair. I am not a taken advantage of 14 year old school girl, drunk on cider at some friend's party. Why am I crying in such amazement?
'It's OK. I think it's a bit of a shock for you. It's early days. You're lucky. You have lots of options. Do you want another tissue? Do you want a termination?'
Do I believe in Hell and Damnation? Or did she say a termination? To terminate. To have a termination. I will be a terminator from here ever after.
Tissues and tears and loud nose blowing noises later.
'I don't know. I don't know what I want. Yes. I know I'm 25. I know I have a partner.' (Does that qualify me?)

PARTNER
- a sharer
- one who plays on the same side as and along with, another in a game.
- person you are with doing something together, e.g. business/dancing/marriage partner.

SLEEPING PARTNER
- one who has money invested in a business but takes no part in its management.

He is not my partner. He is my sleeping partner.

But Doctor believe me, we're not stable, not able to cope, just with the burden of each other. Crazy for each other or just crazy, it'd be madness to make three out of our tumultuous coupling. And Happy Families just isn't what it's all about. But let me out of this surgery, cos I can't breathe in this white bright light and I'm gagging. Is it the stench of anaesthesia?

Do I get a black mask?

'You're obviously taken aback.'

Taken aback? Yes. Take me back to three or however many weeks ago and let me stop this catastrophic event.

'You can see a social worker tomorrow evening when you feel calmer.'

Tomorrow evening I will feel calmer? Why?

'He'll put it all in order for you in your mind.'

Oh no. NO NO. I have to speak to some man about my positive position and the choices I know so well I have. I'm not stupid. Not all the time.

Termination 1: Blood sucking and brief anaesthesia; followed by God knows what. Hopefully amnesia.

Termination 2: Nine month internal body bonding, followed by that humanely fleet snatch at birth; Happy Family Adoption.

Termination 3: Have a baby. Lose a lover and a friend.

Termination 4: Swallow two quick pills and flush it all out of mind and body. Lose a lover and a friend. Watch in surprise as you begin to slide off, round the bend.

Pull yourself back to the white room and listen to the doctor being sensible again.

'It's OK.'

It's OK. It's OK? Really? You think it's OK? I think it's not OK. He'll definitely think it's not OK. And we'll have an un-OK, un-happy family life. OK? What's so OK about all this? Oral contraception is OK, but I'm morally opposed to it. But what are morals now anyway? What is morality and mortality? What is OK?

'You can make an appointment with the receptionist at the front desk.'

The front desk. There's a hotly packed, suspiciously silent waiting room to negotiate before reaching the whispering

receptionist at the front desk. Stripping strip light sullenly illu-
minate the airless room and you're sure all the swift glances
have found you out. You walk with conscious nervous normality. Inquisitive eyes reach out to you across the room. Briefly,
intensely, catch each other's numb stare and both look away
quickly. You, because salty pools are wavering silently over
your whole sparkling eyeball. Gushing river rapids threaten to
burst your deep breathing, brittle thin calm. Him, fear of the
unknown, or the unwanting to know. The refusal to accept
sooner than absolutely necessary. Or just the refusal to accept.
You saw complete denial in that one brief eye conspiracy, but
you deny that you saw it. You are deceiving each other and
yourselves.

> Deceit begins to eat.
> and it has a feast, and grows fat.

Think that tears would let the only conceivable cat out of
the bag to the entire waiting room audience, so stop at two
rolling down your flushed cheeks when the receptionist smiles
sympathetically and calls you softly by your Christian name.
Think of throwing yourself to the lions. Think of throwing
what's now growing inside you to the lions, and jumping in
after it. Whatever it is. Think of throwing your partner and his
smiling face to the lions. Loins. Lions. They all destroy you one
way or another. Wonder why the receptionist is being so understandingly kind to you.

Don't be nice. Don't be nice to me or I'll put my head in
my hands and be swept away in tides of hysteria.

Laboriously make some appointment for the following
evening. Any appointment for anything. Think solely of the
need to leave this overflowing surgery and spill the weight of
this momentous discovery over the other irresponsible half.
You need out into the sweet summer evening with your lover
by your side, to listen to the birds sing and walk home together,
hand in grasping, self-deceiving hand.

He is chatting mutedly to a waiting room companion with
familiar ease that you suddenly want for your own. You look
at him, deep in desperation. He looks up from his conversation. Cuts it thankfully short. Leave the venetian blinded clinic
without looking at each other again. Out in the summer
evening air cry in the fading sunlight. Not even a discreet dis-
tance from the clinic. Arms are supportive and suddenly you're

not alone anymore. Or at least at this moment.

'What happened?' he asks stupidly. Non acceptingly.

I'm crying because it's a normal negative day like any other. Yeh sure. Hell. I wish. You wish.

'It was positive,' you wail pathetically, wanting to be carried home, lain on a huge empty bed, and awoken with a kiss the next morning after a traumatic nightmare.

'What do you mean?'

'I am positive,' you breathe with bewilderment. The only p word you can muster and stomach.

Stagger home leaning on each other. You are a pool of unfathomable water and he is a brick hard stone.

THE DECISION

Reach home and lie in a deceptively soft bed with cups of tea and bars of comforting chocolate to camouflage your confusion. Friends float round your pulsating room clucking with concern and brimming over with well-meant advice. It's uncharted territory for all of you, and no-one says I told you so. No-one makes you feel guilty for what you all know you're thinking. But you do. Termination suddenly presents itself as the only sensible option from the commotion swirling around the island bed that you don't move from. That you're marooned on.

(Since when have I been sensible? Why am I being sensible? Is it for myself?)

Late at night, finally alone together in the silent darkness that surrounds you, grudgingly accept that neither is sleep breathing. Briefly, blindly, hedge around the unspoken, unfamiliar subject of parenthood. Don't do it justice Decide sensibly and quickly on termination and watch in surprise as you are sucked down into a violent whirlpool and he is plucked to a bouncing life raft and the serenity of deep sleep.

4 July 1992

Watch weak grey light creep into the room and finally fall into a soft watery maze of sleep. Dream of fishes swimming interminably in an Indian sea. Curl around your cohort and try to disappear under the covers and through his sleeping body. Wake up minutes later with the sun bursting through the cracks in the blinds and realise it's all too true and not a sleep-drenched mind trick.

Go to work. Teach obnoxious teenagers with a red smile painted on your painstakingly inscrutable face.

Come home. Eat dinner separately, together. Lie on one of the two single beds with a space in the middle that you sometimes feel trapped in. From your bed watch as a tiny white curved summer moon forms in the still sunny sky. Prod your flat stomach. Look at it and convince yourself you feel hungry. At ten to seven he enters the room and you rise from the bed. Realise it hasn't disappeared from his mind, just from both of your mouths and inane conversations. Still unable to touch, glide fat inches apart along the road to the clinic.

At the clinic sit alone in a small windowless room. A man with a beard, beige corduroy trousers and Jesus sandals joins you. It is after all Jesus sandal season. He asks about your decision and you blankly tell the inquisitor that you intend to become a terminator. He nods his head very understandingly and asks you for plausible reasons. You wonder why a man you've never met before is asking you these questions. Meanwhile your head is reeling in an attempt to be sensible again. Serious.

Reasons for termination 1:
It is totally unreasonable. I cannot reason existence out of existence. I have no reason. I am dumbfounded.

Shrug your shoulders and smile hopelessly, staring fixedly at his bushy beard.

'I think you're still very much in shock.'
Really? I don't know.
'Do you feel ready to make a decision?'
Really, I don't know.
'What does your partner think?'
Really. I don't know.

Partner! Cohort in crimes! Please answer this probing inquisitor's questions for me. Even though the decision is singularly mine. Come here and help me!

Bring him into the interrogation room and listen in wished for disbelief as he expounds his inbred Catholic abhorrence for termination. But, what else? His principles can be broken and so can you. Stop listening as the two men wander off into the abstracts of two cars colliding, and thinking after the event as you're lying paralysed in some hospital bed 'What if? If only I'd worn my seat belt I wouldn't be in this situation.' But they've forgotten that this is a situation and not a what if fabrication. Quick decisions waiting to be made. Snap judgements on Judgement Day. But who's judging who?

Leave clutching a written recommendation that you be granted terminator status at the hospital's earliest convenience. Pretend to feel constructive instead of destructive. Wish the whole thing away. Over. Done with.

6 July 1992

Visit the library together. Find yourself mysteriously in the health section holding an old hard-backed book open at the page showing diagrams of foetal development. Stare at the meticulous drawings and read the captions.

Week 1:   Cells are embedded in the wall of the womb.
Week 4:   There is a spinal column
Week 8:   There is a heartbeat.

Stare at the blackness of the words. Find your partner and thrust the book into his face. He looks at you and shakes his head, telling you that you shouldn't be reading it. 'Why are you reading this? You'll only upset yourself.' You wonder what that means. 'There is a heartbeat,' you say, in an attempt to make yourself understood. There is a heartbeat. You wonder if perhaps he has become deaf and blind. But he just walks out of the library and you follow behind, like a dog, silently thinking.

The days drag by with numbing normality. But each day is like a month of melancholy madness.

7 July 1992

Set off alone for a family camping weekend. Sit on a slow moving double decker bus for three hours. Stop at what seems like every village on the east coast of Scotland and belatedly realise that the train takes only one short sane hour. Your mind wanders with the meandering miles and you make a new decision at each remote village bus-stop.

Your friends will be surrogate mothers.

You will carry it in a rucksack round Europe.

You will live in a cottage in one of those picture-postcard, childhood-haven villages and learn to sew and bake.

You are a frantic romantic.

Get off the bus and see your devoted mother and realise that you were being fanciful. Smile winningly; wincingly. Spend the weekend in the bracing seaside air with your fishy secret swimming deep inside you and at the very back of your startled smiling eyes.

9 July 1992

On Sunday night flop exhausted into a train seat and be borne swiftly home to a decisive week.

10 July 1992

Visit the hospital with a willing friend and let the chief gynaecologist probe and prod and again interrogate you. You have cultivated a calm exterior now. Believe you sound convincing and convinced.

Your termination date is fixed. You have a whole week to try to be a normal living person. One who doesn't think. You want to sleep for a week and a day, or else get drunk. But you don't drink. You don't admit the reason why not. Instead, walk about half here and half there inside yourself. Work and lie awake in your single bed beside an empty bed. There's a space where there should be an understanding face. You want a proper discussion of options so he keeps out of your insistently reasoning way, while laughing loudly. Sometimes the noise hurts your ears, other times it's too far away to hear.

THE INTERIM

During the disintegrating days that follow you begin to scream. Silently at first. Then building to a screeching crescendo. You don't know what you're doing anymore. You want to scratch his laughing face.

Finally, lie in one bed talking. Your decision remains but has become mutual. Feel the elastic binding your together tightening. Know it will stretch only a little further. You smile vaguely and vacantly and leave for work.

THE DESECRATION

16 July 1992

Wake up and try to pretend that it's like any other morning. Sit alone in an empty hospital waiting room. Try to reason within yourself, but end up gazing senselessly at the grey wall ahead and feel nothing. Dimly become aware of deep dense uncertainty hammering through your skull. Your consciousness or something ignores it.

Find yourself standing in a stark surgery opposite a man in a white coat. Hear yourself answering 'Yes' when the doctor asks if you're absolutely definitely certain as this is the point of no return. Any other answer would be too long and bear unthinkable consequences. Swallow a pill and swill a glass of chill water. Leave the hospital gladly and spend the airy summer afternoon acting in front of a classful of eager teenagers. Teach them something fun. Feel very full of energy. Be excessively witty. Imagine you can feel strange stomach flutterings, or actually feel them.

Leave school long hours later. Go home and sleep soundly. Don't dream and definitely don't think.

17 July 1992

Return like a wind up toy to the hospital clutching a change of clothes in an innocuous plastic bag. Hope you won't have to use them. Kiss your cohort goodbye for ever and a day and realise finally what it is to be alone.

Walk through the summer morning meadows to the hospital. Look at the green grass and the pink blossom trees. Hear traffic from far off and birds singing from nearby. Have trouble avoiding swooping cyclists. Feel as if you're bouncing along the tree-lined path in a blue balloon. You can't touch anything and everything bounces gently off you; even the warming sunshine.

Reach the hospital. This time sit in a bright sunny television room with coffee and biscuits and a loud woman who wants to talk. Eat a pill each and drink coffee. It's like a coffee morning, whatever that is. The loud woman tells you she has three children. The youngest is only eight months old. She couldn't handle another one. She drones on, animated by her own story; so much so that you aren't called upon to comment or even stay fully upright and awake.

'I'm a regular here love. Doctors think ahm always at it. It's ma husband. He just canny leave me alane. You canny blame im but, can yi'?' You realise you blame him very much because he is half the reason she is sitting here with you. Stare at the wall two inches above her head and switch off as she indulgently embellishes her sex-life saga. Eventually, she doubles over in melodramatic pain and is removed to a hospital bed.

Suddenly your stomach contracts and spasms of pain clench you. Go to the toilet with a tin tray. Curious and masochistic, look in the tray and feel instantly nauseous and disgusted with yourself. Never imagine you'll write about it one day. Give it, genteely covered, to the nurse and begin to sway palely in the corridor. Let the nurse briskly lead you to a hospital bed. Curl up into a tight ball under the scratchy covers and wish for your mum to be sitting beside you stroking your flushed face with a soothing hand.

Realise why you are alone. With a friend, with your mum, with your cohort even, you would have been a watery mass of self pity. This way you can pretend to be someone else; or perhaps just get used to being someone you have suddenly become. Fall into a painful, obliterating sleep.

Wake up in time to go home and feel relieved disbelief that it's all already over. Phone for your partner to collect you. (Why can't you walk home through the park alone? You did the rest of it alone. Is it in case you dissolve on the cool evening grass in a flood of blood and tears?) Wait for him on a hard hospital chair, and fill out a questionnaire about the standard of the hospital's termination service.

Say goodbye to the nurse and furtively ask her, 'Is that it?' She replies that it's all gone and you reflect on whether that's something to celebrate or not. Walk home dually, hand in hand, through the summer evening park. The green grass and pink blossoms are in long cool shadows and you feel like a day has slowly fallen from your grasp, along with something indecipherable and indescribable. Feel glad you didn't need the plastic bag full of clean clothes. Ask mundanely about his day. Answer almost sanely about yours.

In the evening a friend visits and you drink red wine and eat chocolate and laugh vacuously.

Gerry Loose

from STROKE MOTHER

to turn the stone of sorrow to song

shall I say a prayer for you before your death

a novena that you might not know the night yet

the calculations of karma for rest before

an unkaddish of unknown praise untold

a mantra for your motherhood

let me count beads

let me count the little mothers (since I am grown big)

let me count the big mothers (of childhood)

let me lie and say that love destroys death

but I do not believe

120

Roderick MacDonald

SAOGHAL NAN CEARC

Tha na cearcan againne
Gu toirt thairis leis an aois;
Tha iad air fàs deamhnaidh caol,
Is tha gog a' choilich
Air 'leth-ghog'.
Tilgidh Anna thuca dorlach sìl
Is rùsgan a' bhuntàta
Nuair a chuimhnicheas i;
An àite ubh a h-uile latha
Chan fhaigh sinn uatha
Ach aon san t-seachdain;
Tha an coileach mor
Air a dhleasdanas a dhearmad,
'S cha tàinig as a' ghur mu dheireadh
Ach aon isean.
Dh'fhalbh na feannagan leis ...

Nach e saoghal nan cearc
A tha collach ris an t-saoghal.
Chan eil buannachd sam bith
Ann an seann chearcan:
Is cuiridh aon seann chleachdadh
Gun bhuannachd
An saoghal a dhìth ...

Cuimhnich Hioroisioma.

Gordon Meade

THE GUILLEMOT

It came up out of the sea
And fell, exhausted, at his feet.
And the one thought in his head, was
Why, in all the world, did it
Have to come to me?

The bird looked up at him,
Then through him, to a spot behind
His head, to a place it knew it had to
Reach, and wanted to, as quickly
As it could. The breakers

Boomed inside the man's head
Like a drum, and though he wanted
To escape, instead, he found himself
A piece of wood, and knew what
Must be done. He raised

The stick to bring it
Down upon the bird's bowed head,
But missed. The second time, he hit,
And heard the bird's skull split,
And saw its right eye

Flood with blood.
The body twitched, and so, he
Struck once more, and the wooden
Stick and the bird's slim neck,
Snapped in two, as one.

At that moment, he would
Have done almost anything just
To have been able to have got away
From that place, to have found
Himself in a kinder space,

But there he stood,
Transfixed, staring at the
Bird's smashed beak, set somewhere
In between a dead man's grimace,
And a baby's hapless grin.

(From *The Wreck of the Malacca Bridge*,
a sequence)

Ewen Angus MacLean

A'DOL DHAN t-SEARMON RI LA
GEAMHRAIDH O SHEAN

Là na Sàbaid, fon chlaichich,
bodach sneachda, am maor,
na làn fhallus, a'tarraing a'chluig.
As taighean a' bhaile, sean is òg
a'freasdail gairm a' chlagaidh, 's a'toirt
ionnsaigh air fuachd is doineann a' gheamhraidh.

Acaire Dhè fo phlaide thiugh gheal,
Marphaisg ùr thairis nam marbh.
B' e sin geamhradh sa chladh.
Crò gorm càirdeil samhraidh
aìte-còmhraidh roimh adhradh, nis a dhìth,
'sgàth cruadal aimsire, is bagradh taibhseil.

Plosgartach, a'ruigsinn an aitribh
ri siosarnaich teasachaidh on ghas,
gun fheum; fàileadh tinniseach
sgreamhail don t-sròin. Cuid air am fàgail
gun deò a'cuairteachadh ìsleachadh spioraid,
nàmhaid do shùileachadh naomh.

A' chuideachd nan suidhe, 's a' cromadh
snagartaich, 's air chrith, mar losanan
sgàinte nan uinneag. Prìosanach gach aon
an sgoth anail cheòthach fhèin.
Sneachd a' leaghadh om brògan,
'sgaoileadh puill air an làr.

Corragan gorma, reòta, raga dèanamh oidhirp,
a'tionndadh le èiginn nan duilleag,
a'làimhseachadh gu cearbach
anns na pòcaidean tais
buinn dhan Tabhartas.
Gus a bhi deas ann an deagh àm.

Casd is sreathart 'n dèidh a chèile
briseadh sàmhchair làthaireachd.
Cinn gan togail. 'Eisd!'
Motair-rothair aosda a' chlèirich
a'stad le gearan, a-muigh.
'Bithibh modhail, achlann!'
Le ùmhlachd is ùrram tha dòigheil
shealladh an teachdaire dhan chùbaid.
Chuir e dheth an còta mor;
Fo-chòta grinn na Sàbaid a'freagradh
na cùise, geamhradh no samhradh,
gu taghta.

Duine gasda. Fìor Ghàidheal,
èasgaidh, ged air liathadh le aois;
sùilean lorgach, bàidheil, coibhneil
'coimhead thairis an t-sluaigh,
gan gairm on uil' eallachan làitheil,
do shocair is sìochaint an Là naoimh.

'DEANAMAID ADHRADH DO DHIA'
Theich crith, casd is sreathart
gun aire tuilleadh, nas mò
de dh'fhuachd no do theas, 's iad a'seinn,
'Cia taitneach dhomhsa d'Aros naomh,
O Thighearna nam Buadh!'

Audrey Millar

FINDING A VOICE

Every time the dream went a bit further.

Rachel dreamt that she was mountainous pregnant, but instead of being weighted down she floated effortlessly above the rooftops. Her luminous shape hung in the velvety night sky like a Chinese lantern. She felt light and free as she drifted, looking down at the familiar streets lined with tiny houses.

Suddenly sharp needles of pain pierced her and racked her huge body. Still drifting, she pushed against the night and sweat ran into her eyes.

Rachel awoke with a start. As her loud breathing subsided she could hear Tom gently snoring beside her. In faint early morning light she focused on the radio alarm clock. Its cheerful red digits read 5.05 so she rolled over, turning her back on Tom, and drifted back into the darkness.

The kitchen clock showed 8.20 as Rachel cracked the eggs into the frying pan. She sighed as the eggs sputtered in the oil.

'It's time for the traffic news,' she called to Tom.

'More delays no doubt.' Tom was wiping the last traces of shaving foam from his face as he hurried into the kitchen and clicked the radio on.

Thanks for that traffic update Derek, and now over to our newsdesk for the latest national news at 8.30, the radio presenter said as Tom sat down at the kitchen table.

'You look exhausted, dear,' Tom clicked the radio off. 'Haven't you been sleeping?'

Rachel suppressed a yawn as she put the bacon and eggs down on the table.

'I'm fine really,' she said, 'I've just been having a few bad dreams.'

'Ah,' Tom nodded wisely, and she knew what was coming next.

'I never have dreams,' he announced proudly. 'Soon as my head hits the pillow, that's me. Out like a light till morning. ... Perhaps you should try to have a little nap this afternoon, dear,' Tom continued, 'or even better, get out for a nice walk. ... You're not doing yourself any good watching that confounded television all day long.'

'I don't watch it all day,' Rachel tried to control her wavering voice. 'There's a lot of work to be done. I've three loads of washing, and I don't know how much ironing. ... A woman's work is never done. That's what they say, dear.' She tried to look cheerful.

Unheeding, Tom went on briskly, 'If it's not that, it's those magazines, or even worse, those paperback romances you insist on buying... pure trash!' He shuddered.

Rachel watched the clock as they ate in silence.

'Ah well, must be going.' Tom emptied his coffee cup, and pushed back the chair.

'I've got a very busy day today. Three meetings this morning and the Planning Committee in the afternoon.'

He collected his case, and overcoat, and kissed Rachel on the forehead.

'See you tonight then, dear. ... Keep yourself busy, that's the best thing.'

Rachel heard the front door click shut and breathed out. She remained at the table with her coffee, listening to the slow tick of the kitchen clock.

The hands showed 9.05 as Rachel drained her coffee cup. She sighed as she cleared the table and, shuffling over to the sink, she ran the water for the dishes. The day stretched long and empty before her. When the sink was filled up Rachel turned off the tap and noticed with surprise that tiny droplets of water were still falling into the foamy basin. She realised she must be crying.

Later that morning as she sat down at the kitchen table with her third cup of coffee, Rachel glanced at the clock and saw that it was 10.25. Only five minutes till the magazine programme *Good Morning* she thought with relief. She finished her coffee and went through to the living room where she clicked the television set on.

This particular morning was no different from any other. The programme contained the usual mixture of gardening tips, recipes, fashion and discussion of deep-rooted psychological problems by way of the daily phone-in. But initially Rachel found it even more difficult to concentrate than usual. In a trance-like state she absorbed the recipe for Mexican chicken, advice on how to prune rose bushes, the fact that stripes were definitely popular for swim wear this summer, and that you could buy a decent set of garden furniture for around a hundred pounds. The many useless fragments of information began to combine and build. What are the best wines to drink with fresh seafood? How do you go about choosing a hat for a garden party? What should you do if you suspect your teenage child is having a sexual relationship? Rachel was comforted that such questions had answers.

And so it went: should David, who's on the line from Birmingham, tell his wife he's been having an affair? Do blondes have more fun? What kind of weather can you expect if you're planning a barbecue next weekend?

The wave of information continued to rise, until suddenly, gloriously, it broke. As it flooded over and through the corners of Rachel's restless mind, she felt soothed and calm.

11.55 was competition time, and Rachel's trance was momentarily penetrated as she remembered her attempt at entering one of last month's competitions. It had been part of a week of writing competitions the programme had run under the slogan *Finding a Voice*. *Write the opening chapter of a romantic novel, and win a year's subscription to Mills and Boon*, was the enticing offer on that particular day. Rachel had been confident she could do it, after all she had read enough of the things. She had sat all afternoon with an open notebook and pen trying to conjure images of escapism. Words and ideas whirled in her head. Half-sentences formed, fragmented and joined again like a complex jigsaw puzzle.

Student Nurse Forbes noticed Doctor Wood's dark charm during her first time in the operating theatre. His firm masculine hands brushed against her own as she passed him the instruments.

Catherine threw back her waist-length auburn hair and laughed boldly as Sir Edmund dismounted his horse and strode angrily towards her.

The mistral blew across the deserted beach, ruffling her wispy fair hair as she looked out to sea for the returning ship.

Nothing had seemed quite right though, and eventually her mind emptied. After sitting numbly for hours she had been surprised when she looked down at the white page to see one line of her familiar spidery writing.

Wrongness grew in the house like a man-eating plant it said.

Rachel hadn't really understood where it had come from or what it had meant. She had stuffed the torn-off page in the large hat box at the bottom of her wardrobe, beside the empty sherry bottles and forgotten about it.

This week's theme was travel, and today's competition involved identifying various European cities from pictures that were flashed up on the screen. The prize was a weekend break in one of the cities.

She knew that Tom didn't like to travel so Rachel clicked the television set off and went back into the kitchen to load the washing machine.

Seeing it was 12.30 Rachel opened a tin of soup and heated it. She listened to the comforting whir of the washing machine while she sat at the kitchen table eating her soup.

The afternoons were easier since she had discovered a way to block her sadness. Tom had always enjoyed a sherry before dinner, no harm in that, he said. Rachel had found that a few glasses every afternoon could lull her into a pleasant state that was almost like being happy. Of course, this had meant that she had to buy extra bottles, it would never do for Tom to find out. So far, she had managed to find a way to make the money stretch and things had gone smoothly.

She never allowed herself a glass before 1.30, after all she didn't want things to get out of hand. She had seen on television the problems people could have with alcohol if they weren't careful.

After her soup, while Rachel washed up, she glanced anxiously at the clock. When the hands showed 1.30 she scuttled through to the bedroom, opened the wardrobe and took out the hat box which contained an assortment of bottles, some full and some empty.

Giggling to herself, she poured a generous glass, and still carrying the half-full bottle and glass, she went into the living room and sat down in the most comfortable armchair. She didn't feel like watching television this afternoon, or like reading a magazine for that matter. Instead she sat quiet in the chair as sunlight filtered through the venetian blinds and made a pattern on the carpet. The light reflected off her glass, forming a golden brown prism on the white wall. As Rachel watched the patterns of light she had no idea how much time passed; time no longer mattered. She listened to the stillness and drifted.

Every time the dream went a bit further.

This time as her swollen body floated in the blackness the pains were sharper and seemed to last longer. The sky was a rich velvet blanket punctuated with many bright pin-holes of light. Despite the pain she felt happy. She was certain that the baby would soon be born.

Rachel started and listened. She heard a distant jangle of keys, and focusing on the clock on the mantelpiece she saw with alarm that it was 5.30. She knew she had to act quickly. The front door was being pushed open as she drained the glass of sherry and shoved the empty bottle under the cushion on the armchair. She stood awkwardly with the glass behind her back and waited. She could hear Tom was in the kitchen, and then his footsteps grew nearer and the door swung open.

Tom looked cross and slightly dishevelled.

'What's been going on, dear?' His tone was accusing. 'The dinner isn't started, and you don't seem to have managed to hang the washing out. Are you all right?' He sounded concerned, but she felt the irritation in his voice.

'I think I must have fallen asleep,' she said vaguely. 'I'll go and start dinner now.'

Tom marched into the bedroom shaking his head.

Time seemed to drag as they sat in the kitchen, silently chewing. But after dinner things were almost back to normal. The hands on the clock pointed to 7.45 as they sat down in the living room with cups of coffee.

'Fancy the crossword dear?' Tom reached for the newspaper.

It was part of the routine. He always did the crossword in the evening, and usually she helped with one or two clues. Tonight she really didn't feel like it.

'I think I'd rather read my book,' she heard a voice say.

'I don't know why you waste your time with that nonsense.' Tom's tone was gruff as he disappeared behind the rustling newspaper.

Rachel sat quietly and looked at the cover of her book. *Anne Curtis, Junior Nurse* by Mavis Armstrong, it said. The cover depicted Anne; a sweet, but determined, young woman, bending over a patient's bed with concern. Blonde curls peeked out from under her practical nurse's cap. In the background a handsome doctor was gazing at her with interest and admiration.

Rachel opened the book and tried to read. The words seemed like tiny black insects that crawled and wriggled over the page. Large salty tears ran down her face and plopped into the open book. As she wept she was aware of an unfamiliar angry feeling which seemed to be growing inside her. Resentment rose in her throat, threatening to choke her. Tom was chuckling softly at the cartoons page, as Rachel made her way to the bedroom, still sobbing.

Every time the dream went a bit further.

This time Rachel felt sure that she would see her baby, and eager anticipation mingled with her usual contentment as she floated like a luminous balloon over the tiled rooftops. The hot needles began to stab, and red waves of pain surged through her. The velvety blackness was fading and a faint flight grew in the sky. Rachel felt she was falling.

Suddenly she was back in the house, in her familiar bed, and Tom was there. But the pain continued to grow so she kept pushing. Exhausted now, she gathered all her energy up and as she gave one final push she cried out into the night. In a whoosh and surge of water the baby was carried onto the bed below her. Rachel was weak, but tears of joy filled her eyes as she sat up to look. The baby's skin seemed thin and white as tissue paper, and Rachel could see the blue network of veins through it. She wanted to hold the baby, but Tom was lifting it. She tried to cry out in protest but no sound came. Tom was telling her the baby was dead. He said he was sorry, but she knew he had killed it.

Rachel awoke slowly, as grey morning light crept into the bedroom. The tears remained on her face, and as she lay quietly the cold light filled the room. She knew what she must do.

Rachel dressed silently, and, hurriedly, gathered a few things which she stuffed into a carrier bag. The radio alarm's red digits told her it was 5.35. Tom was snoring gently as the front door clicked shut.

Walking down the deserted grey street, Rachel thought about the hat box in the bottom of the wardrobe. She thought about how Tom would find it. About how he would find the empty sherry bottles and the half-full sherry bottles and the torn-off page that she had written on. She thought about it, but she didn't care.

Iain Aonghas MacLeòid

ROINEABHAL

"THA' N T-UISG' A-NOCHD AIR ROINEABHAL
'S THA CEO AIR BEINN A' CHUAILEIN:"
's mo chuimhn' air làithean m' òige nuair
a b' eòlach mi mu'm bruaichean;
dà shreath an sin de dh'òran bha
cho ceòlmhor uair a m' chluasan;
mi 'g èisdeachd ri na h-ògmhnathan
's an clò air cleith ga luadh' ac'.

Bha 'n teaghlach aig mo mhàthair-sa
am Bàigh na Hearadh còmhnaidh,
's dà phiuthar dhith a' tàmh an siud
faisg sàil na beinne bhòidhich:
bha Mairead daonnan bàigheil rium
mar bha a cèile Dòmhnall,
is Raonaid Liath mo ghràdh oirre
's a ghnàth Ian Mòr cho spòrsail.

Bu shona na saor-làithean leam
am Fionnasbhagh 's a' Bhuailidh;
taobh m'athar, cuideachd, càirdean dhomh
an Lingreabhagh na cruaidh-chreig:
's bha Ròineabhal glan àlainn thar
gach àite seasamh uasal;
nach bochd an naidheachd chràiteach dhuinn
is màit' gun toirear bhuainn i.

Gur blàth mo chuimhn' air Ròineabhal
is slògh tigh'nn as gach ceàrna,
a dh'Fhionnasbhagh gu òrdaighean,
gu lòn do'n anam sàsachd:
bhiodh coithional Didòmhnaich fad'
an còrr 'sa ghabhadh àireamh:
is dh'fheumta triall le sòlaimeachd
thar ròid gu lagan sàmhach.

Gu tric am bruadar oidhch' ar leam
mi cluinntinn shailm 'n am mìlseachd;
chi Ròineabhal 'n a greadhnachas,
buan-mhaireannach mar Fhìrinn:
cò chreideadh mur fior-ghloic is e
gun sgoiltear i 's gum mìlltear;
is falamhachd air fhoillseachadh
cur doilgheas air na mìltean?

A.M. Morgan

MY FATHER'S SHOES

My father was a small graceful man with size seven feet. When
he died I was left with his grand piano, his umbrella and his
shoes. Five pairs of well polished brogues – three brown, two
black – which he kept on shoe trees, in a neat row along the
floor of his wardrobe. They fitted me perfectly. I take after my
mother in build, not particularly tall, but square set, with
broad bony feet – a sign of good health according to some
people. My father, hoping for a quiet tractable child, had called
me Violet, but he had named me badly. I was not a shrinking
kind of person. People often drew back in my company, almost
as though I spread invisibly into them.

My father had large eloquent hands that seemed to mirror
his moods. Psychic hands, my mother called them. His fingers
were extraordinarily long and slender with pointed tips, hands
made for playing the piano. I loved to watch him play, marvel-
ling at the fleetness of his fingers, their reflection shimmering
softly in the dark wood. I was jealous of my father's hands.
They were everything he wanted me to be: well-groomed, ele-
gant and artistic. My own hands were clumsy in comparison,
ill-proportioned, with short stubby fingers. Worse still, I used
to bite my nails, a habit which drove my father to the limits of
his patience.

'For goodness sake, Violet, stop that,' he would say, his
hands arching like cats, fingers stabbing into the arms of his
chair.

Other times, sitting with half-closed eyes, his fingers
appeared, impossibly, to lengthen and flatten, so that they
trailed in his lap like pale weed. Then I knew that when he
awoke from his reverie I could ask him to take me to the park,
and he would.

At the age of nine I announced that I wanted piano lessons.
I was keen to practise every day, but the faltering uneven notes
I produced set my father's nerves on edge. It seemed that I
could never please him. He would often appear behind me as I
sat at the piano and proceed to pick holes in my playing.

'Play a bit quieter can't you, Violet? Don't bang the keys
like that.'

My first and only piano teacher was called Miss Quaver.

Evidently her name had influenced not just her choice of career, but also her disposition. It was she who should have been called Violet. Her speech was so soft and hesitant that at times I scarcely dared breathe in case the noise drowned her words. We were mismatched from the start. After I had been learning for about three months, my mother invited Miss Quaver round for coffee one morning, and tried to persuade my father to join them. He refused. He was a person who hated to socialise, but he liked to make an entrance. When my mother returned to the kitchen to get more coffee, the cat sneaked into the back room where Miss Quaver was sitting eating a chocolate digestive. This room was forbidden to the cat, in case it sneezed all over the best furniture, or worse, tried to scratch the piano legs. My father, who happened to be in the hall at the time, grabbed his umbrella and rushed in like one of the Three Musketeers, brandishing his weapon as if to challenge the cat to a duel. The cat immediately fled to a place of safety under the piano, and the next minute my father was down on all fours, shooing it away. I squirmed in my seat, my arms and legs hot and itchy. Miss Quaver had shrunk into the corner of the sofa, pale as a wraith. Having dispatched the cat, my father stood up and turned gallantly to Miss Quaver.

'My apologies if I've made you quiver, Miss Quaver. I simply can't allow that animal to run riot in this room.'

My mother, who had come back in the middle of all this, set down the tray and began to pour more coffee. I ran out and slammed the door, my heart thumping with anger and shame. How dare he humiliate me like this? I heard my mother say,

'For Heaven's sake, Charles, you did that on purpose, didn't you? Just because she'll never play as well as you. It's not her fault you know.'

I climbed the stairs and went to my room. Miss Quaver left shortly afterwards. I couldn't face her again and refused to have any more lessons. My father was right. I was a lumbering beast at the piano, too graceless ever to be any good.

When I was eleven, Sian Murphy, an old friend of my mother's, moved to our area. She had grown up with my mother in South Wales, had married a doctor, and had two daughters around the same age as me. Catherine, the younger girl, was in my class at school, and before long I was spending all my spare time round at the Murphy's house.

I always went in by the back door, through the cramped

gloomy kitchen that led into the riotous clutter of the living room. In one corner stood a standard lamp, its bulb permanently illuminating the faded pink shade. The two small windows of fluted glass allowed little natural light to penetrate the room's dim interior. On the floor in the alcove, beside the dog's dish, were stacked old copies of the National Geographic and the British Medical Journal. Above the dark wooden dresser were five or six shelves, which held books, papers, and a variety of ornaments: several copper lustre jugs, a pair of brass candlesticks fashioned like snakes, and a mock aquarium containing red and blue glass fish. Next to the television was a dining table, its surface usually obscured by more magazines, a fruit bowl and a large chipped pottery ash-tray. Two ancient green armchairs were placed in the centre of the room. The whole place had a murky underwater feel, and smelled of coffee and animal hair.

The rest of the rooms on the downstairs floor were as tidy as the living room was chaotic. We were not often allowed to play in these rooms, because John Murphy, Catherine's father, used them to see patients. Most days he worked up at the local mental hospital, but sometimes he saw patients at his house, and then Catherine and I had to stay in the living room and keep very quiet. It felt odd and slightly thrilling to be under the same roof as a madman.

John Murphy was an Australian of Irish descent. He had a slow shambling gait and thick tanned skin. He reminded me of a rhinoceros. As soon as he met me he started to call me Letty. I had always disliked my name – I never thought it suited me – so I was quite pleased with Letty. Dr Murphy only ever seemed to eat things like soup and yoghurt, and when I asked him why, he said it was because he'd had his stomach removed because of an ulcer, and that kind of food was easy to digest. I found it hard to understand how anyone could manage without a stomach, but John Murphy never seemed to mind me asking questions about it. He even encouraged me. He said I could punch him in the stomach as hard as I liked and it wouldn't hurt him. He used to make the muscles of his belly as hard as a brick, and then urge me to wallop him with my fist.

'Does that hurt?'

'No.'

'Can I do it harder?'

'Go on then.' Thump!

I was amazed that no matter how hard I punched, I never seemed to hurt him.

At weekends I'd usually be lolling about in the Murphy's living room, flicking through magazines and chatting. The air was always opaque with dust and smoke. Sian Murphy smoked filter tips, but John Murphy preferred roll-ups. He would let me roll his cigarettes for him, using a small contraption that looked like a tarnished metal box. I had to feed the paper into the grooved rollers that lay inside the box, line it with tobacco, then close the lid, leaving the gummed edge exposed. I loved to smell the mixture of tobacco and metal as I licked the edge of the paper. Then I would turn the dial at the side of the case, look inside, and take out the completed cigarette. More often than not the television would be on, but nobody paid it much attention. Sometimes John Murphy would pinch his wife's bottom as she walked through to the kitchen, and she would slap his hand playfully. I never saw my own parents lark about in that way. Once, when I was at home watching television with my father, the couple on the screen had started embracing and kissing each other feverishly on the mouth. My father's cheeks had tightened in disapproval, and he had begun drumming his long fine fingers on his knee. I felt my face flush, but at the same time I was fascinated by what was happening on the TV. The kissing seemed to go on for ages. Abruptly, my father got up and switched off the programme.

'I was watching that!' I protested.

He didn't even bother to reply, but stalked silently out of the room and retreated to the seclusion of the piano. I knew that I couldn't disturb him when he was playing.

One Saturday John Murphy said that Catherine and I could play in the front room for a change. It was here that he kept a small record player and his old collection of jazz records. I asked him if I could listen to some of the music.

'OK,' he answered in his slow drawl. 'But if you scratch any of them I'll have your guts for garters!'

The first record we put on was Boogie Woogie piano, with Meade Lux Lewis playing Bear Cat Crawl, and Albert Ammons playing Pinetop Blues. I had never heard anyone play like that before. With its rhythmic bass and jangling melody, I thought it was wonderful. I knew my father would hate it. His taste in music was purely classical. We sat on the floor and worked our way through the pile of albums, the sunshine slicing through the louvred blinds, striping the carpet with bars of dusty light. There was one song by Billie Holiday that we played over and over again, Catherine and I singing along in chorus.

> *When we want to sing we sing,*
> *When we want to dance we dance.*
> *You can do your betting, we're getting*
> *Some fun out of life.*

After this verse came a trumpet solo. Its proud joyous notes seemed to reverberate right through me. We were in full voice, singing the song for the fifth or sixth time, when John Murphy opened the door. He stood for a minute listening to us. When the record had stopped, he said,

'The pair of you seem to like that song!'

'O yes,' I replied. 'Especially the bit in the middle where the trumpet plays!'

'Would you like to have a go at playing the trumpet, Letty?'

'I'd love to! It sounds beautiful!'

He left the room and returned a few moments later, carrying the shiny brass instrument. He sat down in a chair by the window, bathed in the strips of sunlight that made the trumpet gleam silver as well as gold. Handing me the trumpet, he said,

'This belonged to my father. He used to play in a small jazz band in Melbourne. He often said he hoped I'd learn one day, but somehow I've never found the time. Why don't you give it a go? I've a feeling you might be good at it.'

I took the trumpet. It was cold and felt quite heavy.

'Purse your lips together, then blow as hard as you can.'

I lifted the trumpet, put the mouthpiece to my lips, and blew with all my might. Instead of the squeak I had expected, out came a long clear resonant note that died away when I had used up all my breath. I pressed one of the valves down, and the next note emerged warmer and deeper. Altering the shape of my mouth slightly, I blew again and discovered yet another sound.

'That's great Letty!' said John Murphy. 'You're a natural! You can come and play it any time you like. Maybe you could ask your parents to let you have some lessons.'

I couldn't wait to get home. I walked jauntily back to my house, tootling on an imaginary trumpet. A natural, Dr Murphy had said! Maybe my father would be proud of me at last. I ran down the path at the side of our house and went in through the back door. There was no-one in the kitchen. I rushed into the front room and found him sitting reading a newspaper. He glanced at me and grunted.

'Dad! You'll never guess what I've been doing! I've just been round to the Murphy's, and Dr Murphy has got a trumpet, and he let me have a go. It was wonderful – I could play it straight off! Dr Murphy says I'm a natural! So please Dad, can I have some lessons? I really want to learn.'

My father had lowered his paper and was looking at me sternly. His fingers had stiffened slightly.

'I've never heard so much nonsense, Violet. It's a ridiculous idea. The trumpet is not a suitable instrument for a young girl.'

He folded the paper, then took off his reading glasses. I said nothing. He added,

'You gave up the piano, didn't you?'

'But Dad, this is different. I never felt right playing the piano, but the trumpet feels perfect for me! Dr Murphy's father used to play it in a jazz band, and he…'

'That's enough, Violet. I'm not discussing it any more.'

I opened my mouth to protest, but he picked up his paper and strode out of the room, shutting the door with a decisive click. From the next room I heard him strike up the opening bars of a Chopin waltz. I knew then there was no point in arguing. There had never really been any point.

After my father's death I sold the piano. I decided to keep the umbrella and one pair of brown brogues. The others I gave away. The umbrella is black and cumbersome, and the shoes too heavy to wear often. I hardly ever use them, except when I want to feel safe, to arm myself against a sky that is dark with the threat of rain.

Alan MacColl

THE DEAD

When the dead come calling, do we bar the door,
And bolt the shutters, fearful that we may see
Their hats of birch?

Or do we greet them like Canadian cousins,
Build up the fire, pour whisky, turn down beds,
Welcoming them as young men home from war,
Thankful that they're still with us, that by them
We live ourselves?

Liz Niven

IN THE JEWISH QUARTER

In this citie o whispers
Doon daurk, smoky vennels
Windin, we reached the Jewish quarter.
A Golem rins fae the Graveyerd
And the win is reading quate
In the sma synagogue.
Breathin oot the names
Written fae flair tae ruif
O the deid Jews.
Lines loast when Russians
'Restored' the was.
Noo werkmen redraw wi care
These pincil guidelines,
Scrieve again the names –
History rewritten yince mair.

Tony Palombo

HUMILIATION

I saw the defrocked priest
Led through the streets of the village,
Carrying his torn ministry
Clutched in his hands,
Clinging to the rags of his pride
Like an effigy of Christ publicly defaced,
His shame held aloft
In the mock procession.

I saw him wearing the public scorn
Like a crown of thorns
Balanced on top of his head,
Making him tread a path
To his own Calvary
And spread his arms in helpless gestures,
His whimpers rising in the night.

He had transgressed the village mind,
had left his vows behind
In other women's beds,
So now the villagers took their revenge,
Gathered their outrage together
And threw their betrayed faith
Back in his face.

I can remember his tears
When he used to visit my gran,
Before the defrocking,
Tears for his housekeeper
Whom he had loved and buried.

Who was this figure in black
Who dressed like a priest
But behaved like a man?
The answer ran from the town
And disappeared into the ground with his shame.

Torcuil MacRath

SEALLADH

Tha am baile ann gun teagamh. Bha mi ann meall bhliadhn-achan air ais airson seachdain ceann-gnothaich. Chan e baile uamhasach mor a th'ann. Ach tha bùithean agus sràidean ann le càraichean a' siubhal air na sràidean mar ann am baile mòr sam bith eile. Fhads a bha mi ann dh'èisd mi aon fheasgar ri duine ag aithris sgeulachd agus dhùisg an sgeulachd smuain no dha nam inntinn.

Leis an fhìrinn innse rinn mi ana-creideas air na chuala mi agus cha b'e iongnadh a bha sin.cha robh mar a bhitheadh mu cnag na cùise. Ma bha na thubairt an duine ud fior, tha saoghal eile làimh ruinn a bhitheas a briseadh a-steach air an t-saoghal seo o àm gu àm. Bha sin a' dol seachad air sgoilearachd sam bith a bh'agamsa.

Ach 's e an fhìrinn a-rithist gu robh mi eadar dà bharail. Bha ana-creideas ann gun teagamh, ach aig a cheart àm bha beachd math agam nach robh an duine ach ag aithris na chun-naic agus na dh'fhairich e. Mar sin ann a bhith a cur peann ri pàipear fàgaidh mise 'm inntinn fosgailte, cha dèan mi leith-spreidh air taobh seach taobh dhe'n chùis. Innsidh mi an sgeulachd cho math agus as urrainn dhomh, facal air an fha-cal, mar a chuala mi i aig an duine bha siud suas ri fichead bliadhna air ais.

'S e samhradh a bh'ann agus bha am baile laghach. Thuilleadh air a sin bha na daoine càirdeil, faisg dhuit nan dòighean mar bu dual do na Gàidheil. Bha nàbachd ann aig an àm ud, 's dòcha nach eil ann an diugh. Bha gu sònraichte dithis anns a' bhaile air an d'fhuair mi deagh eòlas agus air feasgar brèagha chaidh sinn le chèile gu drama.

Cha mhor nach robh an taigh-seinnse falamh. Bha an triùir againne nar seasamh ris a' chuntair is bha grunnan beag eile pìos bhuainn. Cha robh an còrr fo na cabair ach a-mhàin a' chaileag òg a bha air taobh eile a' chuntair. Cha mhotha na sin a bha ceòl ann, ach cha robh am feasgar ach òg. Bha an t-àite samhach. Mar sin chualas fuaim an doruis nuair a nochd an duine bha seo a-steach.

Bhitheadh e mu shia troighean de dh'àirde no 's dòcha beagan goirid air a sin, a' streap suas ann am bliadhnachan chanainn, ged nach robh e ga shealltainn. Bha e fhathast seang

mun mheadhan agus dìreach san druim le ceum làidir aige.
Bha e na aodach obrach le slat thomhais a' nochdadh a-mach
air bàrr na pòcaid. Feumaidh e bhith gu robh an obair-latha
seachad. Thug e sùil aithghearr mun cuairt air mus tàinig e a-nall
chun a' chuntair. Sheas e làimh ruinne is dh'òrdaich e tomhais
de dh'uisge-beatha agus glainne portair. Chuir esan agus an
dithis a bha còmhla riumsa fàilte air a chèile.

Leis a sin thòisich a cheithrir againn a'bruidhinn a-null 's a-
nall fhads a bha a chaileag a' lìonadh na drama agus a' tarraing
a' phòrtair.

Ach an seo agus an còmhradh air a dhol caran fann, thubhairt esan as a ghuth – thàmh. "Thachair rud dhomhsa anns a'
mhadainn an-diugh a chaidh fada, fada seachad air a bheagan
tuigse a th'agam-sa. Chan e fear-eaglaise a th'annam", ars'
esan, "ach ged a b'e gu dè am fios a tha aig sagart no aig minis-
tear seach duine sam bith eile."

"Chan eil oidhche ann an-drasda", ars' esan. "Chunna mi
nuair a dhùisg mi ann an solus na maidne, boireannach le
aodach geal oirre a' gluasad air falbh bho thaobh mo leapa
agus a' dol as an t-sealladh. Ghlac mi", thubhairt e, "aiteal dhe
h-aodann ach chan urrainn dhomh a' radh le cinnt sam bith
gum faca mi i a-riamh roimhe siud".

"Ach bitheadh sin mar a dh'fhaodas" ars' esan "ach 's e a
th'agam ach am faireachdainn math a bha coise an t-seallaidh.
Chan eil e furasda còmhradh a chur air ged a tha dà chànan
agam. Chanainn gu robh mathas a' drùidheadh a-steach orm
agus", ars' esan "tha mi a' dèanamh dheth gur e sin a dhùisg
mi. Co dhiù, chan urrainn duine a' dhol as àicheadh na chì
agus na dh'fhaireas e".

Fhreagair fear dhen dithis a bha còmhla riumsa anns a'
bheurla – thuigeadh e Gàidhlig ach 's ann lapach a bha e ga
bruidhinn – "seach gur e sealladh math dhutsa a bh'ann na
cuireadh e uallach sam bith ort. Gu cinnteach", thubhairt e,
"tha daoine a faicinn seallaidhean ged nach fhaca mise càil
dhen t-seòrsa a-riamh. Tha an tiomradh", ars' esan "a' tighinn
a caochladh àiteachan air feadh an t-saoghail".

Cha deach an còrr a ràdh mun chuspair. Thionndaidh an
duine bh'ann ris an stuth a bha e air a cheannach. Cha do chuir
e beul air fhads a bha e a' bruidhinn. Bha a' chaileag a bha air
taobh eileden chuntair a' coimhead air le uabhas ach cha dubh-
airt i smid. "Feumaidh mi", ars' esan, "cabhag a dhèanamh, 's

ann a tha mi air an t-slighe dhachaidh agus chan eil dad agam
mu dheidhinn a bhith ag òl 's a dràibheadh".

Cha b'fhada as dèidh sin gus na dh'fhalbh an duine agus
bha mise a' fàgail a' bhaile an ath latha. Chaidh faisg air fichead bliadhna seachad mus fhaca mise am baile ud a-rithist. Ach
ged as neònach an rud e, dh'fhuirich an sgeulachd an àiteigin
air cul m'inntinn 's gun mi a' dèanamh oidhirp chruaidh sam
bith gus a' cumail air chuimhne.

Mar sin nuair a ruith na bliadhnachan agus a thill mi don
bhaile ud, thàinig an sgeulachd gu m'aire. Chuir mi romham
gum faighinn còmhradh air an duine aig an cuala mi i, ma bha
e fhathast beò. Mar a bh'anns a' fhreasdal bha e fhathast an
làthair ged nach robh a' cheum a-nis cho làidir no a dhruim
cho dìreach 's a b'àbhaist. Mhothaich mi gu robh an inntinn
cho beòthail 's bha i a-riamh.

"An gabh sibh drama", dh'fhaighnich mi dha, "tha botal
agam anns a' chàr", "S e mo charaid a bheireadh dhomh i",
fhreagair e, ach cha ghabh mi ach aon". Nuair a shuidh sinn
sios gu dòigheil dh'innis mi dha fath mo thurais, gu robh mi
airson bruidhinn air sgeulachd a chuala mi aige anns an taigh
sheinnse bliadhnachan air ais. "Bheil cuimhne agaibh",
dh'fhaighnich mi.

"Tha", fhreagair e, "fàgaidh sealladh dhen t-seòrsa ud
làrach air inntinn duine". "An tug e buaidh air ur beatha",
dh'fhaighnich mi a-rithist. "Thug" ars' esan, "anns an t-seadh
's gu bheil mi a' creidse nach ann aig an t-saoghal seo a tha am
facal mu dheireadh idir. Tha a' bheatha a tha againn nas fhar-
sainge na sin". "Ach", ars' esan, "ge be air bith gu dè a chì no
chluinneas duine bu chòir dha inntinn fhèin a ghleidheadh. Sin
am beachd a bha agam a-riamh agus cha tàinig caochladh air".

Dh'innis mi dha gu robh dùil agam an sgeulachd aige a'
sgrìobhadh sìos ach cha robh e airson gum bitheadh an t-ainm
aige air an duilleig idir. Bha e a' cumail a-mach gu robh an
sealladh pearsanta dha fhèin. Mar sin thubhairt mi ris gum
fàgainn an t-ainm aige agus ainm a' bhaile falaichte.

Anns an dealachadh thubhairt e rium, "Nuair a bhitheas
an sgeulachd sin agad air paipear, thig air ais an seo gun fhios
nach toir mi sgeulachd eile dhuit".

Richard Price

AS, AS

What falls between us
is the rain
as thick as, as fast as,

and you're there with your ornaments
and we're here with our tucked-up nets
(say the car-park dividing us joins us),

and the snow
is just heavier than leaves,
just more liquid,
plural as millions et cetera –

it's as fluid I mean
as creamy falling stars

and what falls between us
falls and finishes the.

'Bye' I say, say,
and all of us, well, wave.

IN THE PARISH OF KILFILLAN

With his rucksack in the back
the hitchhiker brought you luck:
you drove the gorse-lined road
and the spikes didn't touch.
St Fillan and the stricken tree,
Warlock Road and the well of keys,
made you belong with them.

Three/four miles and his bonny talk
had done the missionary work:
he drove the gorse-lined road
and the fox was by the birch.
St Fillan and the stricken tree,
Warlock Road and the well of keys,
made you belong with them.

The fox was by the birch,
a mare by the hedge and curve:
he drove the gorse-lined road,
he made the living swerve.
St Fillan and the stricken tree,
Warlock Road and the well of keys,
made you belong with them.

The gain is in the grit.
The creatures knew the cut
granted by the gorse-lined road,
and the thorns did much.
St Fillan and the stricken tree,
Warlock Road and the well of keys,
made you belong with them.

Climb out the leafy wreck.
The driver is a rowan stick
planted by the gorse-lined road
and the saint inflamed the switch.
St Fillan and the stricken tree,
Warlock Road and the well of keys,
made you belong for them.

Kenneth C. Steven

GLEANN MO SHEANAR

Gleann mo sheanar
Far an robh e beò mus do gheàrr rathaidean
Clàr an t-saoghail ùir.

B'aithne dha far an laigheadh am bradan
Anns gach glumaig a bha a'lasadh
Airgeadach le tuil na Dàmhar.

B'aithne dha cuairt na h-iolaire
Mar phìos maide anns an adhar bhalbh,
Cuairt an rìgh.

B'aithne dha lùb na fidhle
Agus lorgadh e ri ciaradh feasgair
Fuinn ris an dèanadh casan danns'.

THE GLEN OF MY GRANDFATHER

The glen of my grandfather
The place he lived before roads
Cut the map of the modern age.

He knew where the salmon lay
In every pool that flashed
October flood and silver.

He knew the eagle's spread
Like wood in still-cut sky
The circling of a king.

He knew the fiddle's bend
Could find among the evening's dark
Tunes to dance the feet.

THE LONG SILENCE

On Iona the last Gaelic speaker has died.
Last winter when the gales battled each roof and window
He was blown out and into the wind.

Once upon a time he was a tall man
Leaning at the porch of his weaver's cottage
His eyes like pools of the sea.

Now in the summer when the tourists come
You will hear the languages fast and loud –
But never a word of Gaelic there.

All over the western islands, the last ones are going
Like candles tonight, falling across the wind,
Their last words lost and drowned in time.

But everyone is talking, busy talking,
The radios and televisions are loud all night
And no-one is listening to the long silence.

Ruth Thomas

THERAPEUTIC

I sit with my head almost leaning against the window, but the glass is smeared and I don't let myself touch it, not even the tips of my hair. I want to get out of this train. I want someone to kiss me and carry my luggage. A beige plastic cup is rolling towards me. It leaks bits of coffee when the train swings outwards.

On the other side of the table a man is doing a tapestry. He has been doing this tapestry for two hundred miles. Since Doncaster. It is in a big wooden frame, which I imagine he hammered and sawed into shape like a thin Father Christmas making a sleigh. Maybe he has a wife who comes in with Ovaltine. Maybe he has a cat. The tapestry is sparkling: gold, yellow, bronze, and he is stitching small squares. He is wearing a checked shirt and crepe-soled shoes.

Outside a man walks along the river bank in a flat cap. He always seems to be there when I look out of train windows; I feel as if I should wave. The sky is white and cold. October. I look back into the compartment. Red and grey lines intersecting; a chain in a box, penalty for misuse £50. The automatic door has gone wrong and opens all the time. People walk past: crimplene backsides occasionally followed by children's heads. There is a smell of cheese from the buffet. The tapestry man sighs, puts his hands inside a plastic bag and chooses some more thread. Silver.

'So,' he says, and I jump.

'So,' he says, 'what are you studying?'

'Well,' I say, 'I'm not studying. I used to study, but I don't study any more.'

'Yes,' says the man, 'you look like someone who would study something.'

'Do I?' I say, then I laugh, high and false, and stare quickly out of the window. The man sucks the end of the silver thread, picks up his needle, and the thread bends for a few seconds before going through. For a while the train is quiet: I can just make out a Roxy Music song playing through someone's Walkman. The train slows down as it goes through a small station, but not slow enough for me to see the name on the platform. I know the man is going to say something else any minute. I am waiting for another comment. I don't like talking on trains: I like being silent, but this man wants to talk. He draws breath; I get ready to make a response but he doesn't say anything. Then he draws another breath and says,

'Very therapeutic, embroidery.'

'Yes,' I say.

'Do you sew at all?'

'A bit of darning sometimes. I used to embroider when I was younger.'

'But you are not old now,' says the man.

'No,' I say, 'not that old.'

'A spring chicken,' says the man, 'a mere slip of a girl.'

'Mmm,' I say, and try to adhere my gaze closer to the view, as if I am suddenly interested in a factory outside called the Universal Grinding Wheel Company Ltd. My hair touches the glass. It is cold outside. When I pull my hair round my shoulder, it leaves wispy imprints in the condensation.

'Travelling far?' says the man.

'Up to Edinburgh,' I say.

'I am getting off at the next stop,' says the man. 'I shall have to start packing up my bits and pieces in a minute.'

'I expect that takes a while,' I say. I want to be friendly now – now I know that we will not be travelling the next 150 miles together.

'I am going in for a competition,' says the man. 'We have to design a church hassock.'

He turns the frame round and holds it up for me to look at. There is a big square of empty canvas in the centre, and a few rectangles around it.

'I have a long way to go,' says the man. 'It is meant to say *Consider the lilies of the field, how they grow, they toil not, neither do they spin*, but I have to send it off by next Tuesday so I think I'm going to have to shorten it.'

'Right,' I say. 'Maybe just *Consider the lilies of the field* will be enough,' I say, 'Because I think most people know it anyway, you know, the general gist.'

'Ah,' says the man, 'but is the *general* gist good enough for a church hassock?'

I can't think what to say. There is something strange about this man, as if he wants other people to hear him. He turns the frame round again and starts to pull thread through the canvas. It makes a pulling noise. I like the sound – it is precise, like a cat purring.

I have with me a laundry bag full of apples. They are bulging in this big flowery bag. On trains there is nowhere to put things like this. To prevent seven pounds of fruit from rolling around the carriage, I have had to tuck the bag behind my legs. I get one of the apples out of the bag, examine it for bird-pecks, then bite into it. It is cold against my teeth, and almost white inside. The apple is a little misshapen, slightly off-centre, but it tastes good.

'An apple a day,' says the man, snapping thread between his teeth, 'an apple a day keeps the doctor away. I wonder how old that saying is?'

'Mm,' I say. There is a tiny fleck of apple between my two front teeth.

'These old sayings often make a lot of sense,' says the man.

The train starts to slow down. A man with a stammer says *Newcastle. Newcastle will be the next station stop.* The tapestry man starts to put away his threads. He wraps them round his fingers and makes short skeins, then he puts them one by one into his plastic bag; gold, silver, yellow.

'Nearly there now,' he says. 'Nearly home.'

'It looks as if it's raining out there,' I say, trying to peer through the smears on the window. It is getting dark. On the seat behind me there is a little girl talking to her mother. 'Look at the lights,' she says, 'they look like birds, golden birds flying.'

'I think you are hallucinating,' says her mother.

The man says, 'I hope the rest of your journey goes well.' He is still talking in a loud voice, as if he is on a stage. He turns his head to look at the other passengers. When he moves the tapestry frame, I see he has nearly finished the C of Consider. There is also something that looks as if it might be a lily in the top left-hand corner. The man smiles and says, 'I have my work cut out for me.'

'I've got about seven pounds of apples here,' I say suddenly. I don't know what makes me say this. 'Would you like one?' I say.

'No. No, I won't, no thank you,' he says, 'they give me indigestion. I *need* a doctor if I eat apples.'

He laughs with his mouth wide open. He picks up his tapestry frame. 'Goodbye,' he says. 'So nice to have met you.' He waits for the shuffle of people to go past then proceeds through the automatic door, which is now permanently wedged.

I watch him walking down the platform, with his frame and his bag of threads. The little girl behind me is singing, 'Bye bye Newcastle'. Then it's just me and this bag of apples. For some stupid reason, I feel lonely.

Sheena Thomson

PIGGY LEGS

'Thunder thighs!' you'd call
as I toiled in those navy shorts.
You'd wonder aloud
as I hurried down corridors,
how I crammed my trotters into
those clacking little shoes.
I weighed nine stones.

It was possible to avoid lunch
by taking up smoking.
I weighed eight stones and two pounds.

I never wore jeans, or mini-skirts,
or flat boots.
So I never went hill-walking,
or sailing, or swimming.
Or did anything that couldn't
be done in a long black skirt.

Living alone,
it was easier to miss breakfast.

There are 400 calories in lasagne for one.
There are 560 calories in apple crumble.
There are 190 calories in a packet of crisps.
I weighed seven stones and ten pounds.

'You've a pretty face,' he said,
'even if you have got thick ankles.'

There are 90 calories in an apple.
There are 40 calories in a slice of turkey.
Next to nothing in a strawberry
– and coffee is always better black.
I weighed six stones and five pounds.

Swallowed food clings under skin
in clotted, ugly lumps.

My hair breaks,
I keep its dullness short.
My teeth have holes,
ache with heat or cold.
My breath stinks.
I haven't bought Tampax for two years
I weigh five stones

and I have fat legs.

Ruaraidh MacThòmais

IAIN GRIMBLE (1921–1995)

Nuair a thuit thu aig bun na staidhre
dh' fhairich ar n-eachdraidh an grèim;
ged a bha an rathad fada
bho Hong Kong, troimh Winchester
is Ath-nan-damh is Lunnainn,
ràinig thu Dùthaich Mhic Aoidh
is dh' fhàg thu làrach innt'
a mhaireas.
Bha do bhodhaig làidir
's do chridhe dìleas
chun na mionaid mu dheireadh,
do pheann a' freagairt d' inntinn
le leum-àrd
's do bhuille-snàmh
a' sgathadh uisgeachan buairidh
's a' fàgail soilleir ás do dhèidh.
Tha fhios gun cuir Rob Donn fàilt ort
ma thachras sibh ann a saoghal eile,
's bidh sgeulachd no dhà agaibh
mu Shrath Nabhair 's Gleann a Gallaidh.
Dhuinne, a th' air ar fàgail,
gus an tig am beum
bidh cuimhn' againn air d' uaisleachd
's air do ghàire
's air sgaiteachd do sgeul.

Derick Thomson

IAN GRIMBLE (1921–1995)

When you fell at the foot of the stair
our history felt the pain;
though it was a long road
from Hong Kong, via Winchester
and Oxford and London,
you reached the MacKay Country
and left a mark there
that will last.
Your body was strong
and your heart true
to the last minute,
your pen answering your mind
with a high-jump,
and your breast-stroke
splitting the waters of contention
and leaving clear water behind you.
Undoubtedly Rob Donn will welcome you
if you meet in another world,
and you will exchange stories
about Strath Naver and Glen Gollaidh.
For us, left here,
until the stroke comes
we will remember your nobility
and your laughter
and the cutting-edge of your story.

Valerie Thornton

THE WORD IS WHITE

My head's bursting with colours today. Mostly blue.

The waiting room was full of people with people. Mothers with daughters, daughters with mothers and women with men. That and an air of tension although the place looked mostly like a busy department lounge. Women were called every minute or so.

And I am alone, dressed in blue, because I thought it might calm me down a little, with pearly shell buttons from the blue sea, and Indian mirrors on a blue embroidered waistcoat to ward off evil. I couldn't sit, because there were no seats left so I walked slowly around the outside of the square part and pretended to read the leaflets and helpline numbers. So many things that can be wrong. At least I only had one.

Then they called me to a corner room and told me to strip to the waist, and put on the gown – one of these ridiculous, stiff, paper goonies with ties like vilene. And bright blue, like forget-me-nots. Hopeless. I assumed they wanted the gashed opening at the front.

Professor Bernard – a doubly blue name with the P and the B – was avuncular, and put his hands, his warm hands, straight onto my breasts. He found it too, and rolled it thoughtfully between his fingers.

'Probably not, because it's painful,' (blue) he said, 'and mobile,' (pale blue). 'But we can do a biopsy (again blue). It'll be back from the Path Lab (blue) in twenty minutes.'

Please – blue – please.

And he trapped the pain hard between his fingers and flared it beyond red into black with the brightness of the needle, coring the pain into calibrations of maybe. Somewhere in the middle he asked about my work, but I was beyond words in this black and silver fire. And then it came out and went out.

'Give me your left hand and hold it here, on the pain,' he said. 'Go when you are ready, and wait and I'll come and get you. I'm sorry to have hurt you,' and he laid his arm briefly from my breast bone to my belly. Comforting. He gave me a tissue and left.

Together, I waited, as the pain began to diminish towards a merely blue word. The place had ginger stone arches, and a roof with windows and arched wooden girders, kingfisher green, and looked from below like a swimming pool, but only sunlight poured around us and cool air falling from the whirling fans.

I don't remember his words but they were good ones. And, with it shrinking, I may not need the knife after all. 'Come back in three months. I'm sorry to have hurt you.' And he took my hand then held my eyes and left.

And all I feel is drained. Not pleased, which is blue, or anything. I thought I was dead already.

In the evening I find myself finishing things because I can start again tomorrow – sewing the last lace cuff onto a cotton sweater, heavily patterned and blue, and threading the ends away. And completing a necklace of blue beads – navy and royal and pale royal but nothing turquoisy or greenish. Intensely blue, real blue.

As I pack all the seed beads away afterwards, I tip a box onto the carpet. Everywhere, tiny blue glints. Now I have time again and I pick up each one, hunting with my fingers after my eyes have done their best.

And, as the twilight fades to milky blue, I should have known. After all the word is white, vicious and cold, and very distant now.

Anyway, my favourite colour is not blue, but green: the colour of wounds and warts and wens. And worry.

Gael Turnbull

A BIT PART: FROM CHEKHOV

not even a walk-on – a voice from behind a backdrop – not
even words – but calling something – summons? greeting?
directions? – and Cherbutykin: 'That's Skvortsov, the second,
shouting from the boat'

before the duel, before the Baron is killed, off stage, a fool
anyway – who wasn't meant to be killed, just frightened,
grazed – but however careful, a bullet is a bullet – and
Skvortsov

must have had to deal with the body, tell the family, sort it
out – and Cherbutykin, later: 'What does it matter?' – and
Olga: 'If only we knew, if only…' – what isn't in the script

or of what happened to Skvortsov – after the curtain – who
remembers, if nothing else, as no one else – being there,
unseen, unable to see, listening for his cue, ready

to call out in the silence – to make it matter, understandable,
what Cherbutykin would say – and then, whoever – and so
on – and perhaps even Olga – what only Skvortsov – alone in
the dark – only he knew – he knows.

Brian Whittingham

THE PARISIAN STRONGMAN

The Parisian strongman
wears overalls
over his strongman's hairy chest.

Like gunfire
his whip cracks the air
trying to extinguish the cigarette
he has placed in a young man's mouth.

He tells his victim
'No need to worry
the hospital is only ten minutes away.'

He clatters Americans on the head
with his caveman's rubber club.
He throws a cannonball
that crashes onto the concrete
then throws a sponge replica
into the crowd
who duck and dive for cover.

The strongman's whiskered face
breaks out
into his showman's grin.

He pulls a beautiful young woman
from the crowd
revealing a giant condom.

The Italians clap and whistle
as he chastises a German
who clunked a few measly francs
into his tin chamber pot.

And as he lurked upon passing women
pinching their bottoms
with wolf whistles and bravado.

his lanky assistant;

who had sorted out
the escapologist's chains
the juggler's knifes
and the bed of nails

balanced a lethal looking sabre
on the point of his pointed chin
and strolled about
as if it were the most natural thing
to do.

Kevin Williamson

MURDER IN GLASGOW

There was never the poem
that needed introduction.

Like this one. Set in its own
concrete shoes on the floor

of The River Clyde gubbling out over
Glasgow. Its mouth is closed.

Like the yards like the private gardens.
Its tale takes a lot to swallow.

Time after time there are bubbles
of thought to the surface.

Continue, they glug, continue to flood
this town with all that it seeks.

O Taggart. You will never find a person
in this poem who has a clue.